FRIENDSHIP
A. C. GRAYLING

YALE UNIVERSITY PRESS
NEW HAVEN AND LONDON

VICES AND VIRTUES
Series editors Richard G. Newhauser and John Jeffries Martin

Copyright © 2013 A. C. Grayling

First published in paperback in 2014

For information about this and other Yale University Press publications, please contact:
US office: sales.press@yale.edu www.yalebooks.com
Europe Office: sales@yaleup.co.uk   www.yalebooks.co.uk

Set in Sabon MT by IDSUK (Data Connection) Ltd
Printed in Great Britain by Hobbs the Printers Ltd, Totton, Hampshire

Library of Congress Cataloging-in-publication Data

Grayling, A. C.
   Friendship / A. C. Grayling.
      pages cm
   ISBN 978-0-300-17535-6 (cloth : alk. paper)
1. Friendship. I. Title.
   BJ1533.F8G625 2013
   177'.62—dc23

2013021868

A catalogue record for this book is available from the British Library.

ISBN 978-0-300-20536-7 (pbk)

10 9 8 7 6 5 4 3 2

FRIENDSHIP

A. C. GRAYLING is founder and master, New College of the Humanities, London. A multi-talented and prolific author, he has written over thirty books on philosophy and other subjects while regularly contributing to *The Times*, the *Financial Times*, the *Observer*, the *Literary Review* and other publications. He is also a frequent and popular contributor to radio and television programmes. He lives in London.

amare curare sentire refovere osculari oblectare tangere fortunare

Contents

Contents

Acknowledgements

My thanks go to Dr Hannah Dawson, who read the manuscript and made illuminating comments, Tosca Lloyd, who researched the references and bibliography, my other colleagues and students at the New College of the Humanities, London, the librarians at the University of London library, the London Library, the British Library, and the editorial staff at Yale University Press, for help and many acts of friendship ranging from the practical to the inspirational.

Foreword
Richard G. Newhauser and
John Jeffries Martin

It is altogether fitting that the series 'Vices and Virtues' should begin with *Friendship*. As A. C. Grayling's inaugural volume amply demonstrates, friendship describes the finest of human relationships: a lasting bond that transcends whatever accidental or utilitarian reasons might have brought two people together in the first place. One can debate with a friend without quarrelling; one can argue with a friend as a matter of discussion, not dissension. This is, of course, the presupposition of Socratic dialogue; it underlies any idea of progress in politics as well. And opening this kind of reasoned debate on matters of contemporary ethics is one of the goals of our series. But this is not to say that the virtue of friendship is a matter of Platonic realism: it has a history, and that history, as Grayling observes, has led to debates about what exactly constitutes friendship or, at times, whether individual friendship should be given preferential treatment in the network of relationships in a community. The history of ethical conceptions, their varying valences in changing social and cultural situations, constitutes another important element in the goals of the series that begins with this volume.

'Vices and Virtues' will come to constitute a library of ways of thinking historically about ethics. For our age, ethical thought is no longer comprehensible through foundational arguments; rather, ethics is most fruitfully approached historically, with sensitivity to the social, political and cultural contexts that shape moral values and lead to new moral visions over time. One of the most challenging aspects of a history of ethics is that moral values often stand in tension with the culture in which they emerge. A particular theory of justice, for example, may challenge the very structures of the society in which it is first articulated. A concept of individual friendship may be at variance with the universal aspirations of Christian *agape*. Thus, not only does ethics have a history; the relation of ethics to history is a subject rich in the possibility of intellectual discovery. Moreover, this is a realm of enquiry that cries out for exploration – especially at a time such as our own when the language of morality is manifestly in need of precision. One has only to listen to the word 'friend' in the mouth of contemporary politicians referring to someone in a different party to see both how expected, even desired, the discourse of friends seeking solutions to political problems is today, and how hollowed out the idea of this virtue has become in the arena of politics.

The key terms in the title of the series are used in an expansive sense to bring to the foreground a set of topics that is of contemporary interest. Readers of the series might expect to find books devoted to traditional vices such as lust, lying and envy, or traditional virtues such as faith, justice and hope, but they can also expect to see volumes devoted to issues not normally included in the traditional lists. What will give unity to the series is its commitment to examine moral issues from a historical perspective, with attention to how the cultural understanding of each category has shifted over time. But what the reader can also expect in contributions to 'Vices and Virtues' are volumes in which clarity, breadth of vision, and especially the talent to engage a broad range of readers in reasoned discourse are essential elements. One can find no better example of all these elements than A. C. Grayling's analysis of friendship and its history.

Introduction

The highest and finest of all human relationships is, arguably, friendship. Consider the fact that we regard it as a success if we become friends with our parents when we grow up, our children when they grow up, our classmates or workmates even as they remain classmates or workmates, for in every such case an additional bond comes to exist, which transcends the other reasons we entered into association with those people in the first place.

And of course our friendships with people who do not fall into one of these categories – that is, our friendships with people who were strangers beforehand – are special in a different and typically less complicated way, because they are purely elective; we meet someone and take a liking to him or her which is reciprocated, and thereafter we enjoy each other's company, laugh together, share interests and views, and over time come to feel that we are part of the fabric of each other's worlds, a valuable part, so that we develop a mutual sense of obligations owed and trust given, and meet each other's needs for boon companionship, comfort, confidences and sharing. And we do all this to such an extent that if we lose such a friend we feel the loss deeply, as of someone loved. Indeed we talk of loving our friends, or some of the closer among them anyway, and their loss can accordingly be profound.

When I think of the friends I had when young, and of the friends made in the course of work and endeavour, of the evenings in their company or on long journeys, of the things learned and shared with them, of the burdens halved and the sorrows comforted – and above all the laughter enjoyed, I realise that it is only the supremest moments of the intimacy of love that can compare in value to friendship – and even then we hope that, in the ideal, the former will be a prelude to the latter for the rest of our days.

Different people provide the friendship we need at different times in our lives, even if certain very particular friends stay the whole course. This is a reflection of the fact that most people change with time and experience, and since all parties to a friendship are changing simultaneously, it is not surprising that they might eventually drift apart. In adult life such drift is accelerated when people take sides with one of a divorcing pair – and sometimes people who were friends with a couple lose touch with both of them when they separate.

These are among the facts of contemporary friendship, but they only scratch the surface, because the interplay of moral psychology, emotion, the changing patterns of family and working lives, shifting relationships between the sexes, the effect of religion and its decline as a controlling force in many societies, the models offered by film and television, the wider scope for friendships and relationships in adolescence, the effect on these of electronic social media, and much besides, make the already highly complex phenomenon of friendship even more confused and diffuse.

Indeed the words 'friend' and 'friendship' have become so stretched and extended as to have lost a good deal of their meaning, and this even before we begin to ask for lines of demarcation between friendship and other relationships, and before we ask in what sense there can be friendships across sexes and ages, cultures and ethnicities, divides of experience and oppositions of attitude. Of the famous friendships recorded in history and legend, most are between men and most of these in turn appear not to be friendships as such but homosexual loves, which raises the question whether much of the thinking about friendship in classical antiquity and afterwards is about a very special and intense version of it, focused upon erotic attraction and its fulfilments. Might this not mislead us in thinking about ideals of friendship, given our intuition that it is something significantly different from passion and desire? These latter form the alembic in which biological imperatives so easily supplant social and psychological interests, which some argue are the true domain of friendship while the sexual imperatives underlie another story altogether. Is that right? Must lovers and spouses move on from that bond before friendship supervenes? Another intuition rejects this thought.

And yet: like love, friendship is a matter far more of emotion than rational calculation. Indeed if it is wholly or even largely the latter, we scarcely think that it merits the name. Of course there are considerations of mutual benefit, help, advantage and support implicit in the idea of friendship, but generally these

are the sequelae of the engagement of emotion which constitutes friendship, rather than the motivations for it. For when
these are indeed the motivations for one person to seek friendship with another, we are instinctively suspicious; we talk
of a person so befriended as 'being used', of insincerity,
untrustworthiness; we talk of false friendship, in which the
seeming-relationship is a hollow matter because something
essential and fundamental is missing. To identify this essential
and fundamental thing is to understand at least what lies at the
core of the relationship, and we can be cheered by the reflection
that since we are very clear about when it is lacking, we should
be somewhat clear about what it is. It cannot be hard to find the
focus of the concept, even if what ranges away on all sides into
variety and particularity covers much territory.

Nor is it too hard. Essential and fundamental to friendship
is that it is a natural, spontaneous, freely given and entered into
relationship premised as much on subliminal cues that prompt
liking as on anything that the parties could specify as a reason
for engaging in it. Such reasons would *ex post facto* doubtless
abound: shared interests, attitudes, views, taste, style, appearance, behaviour, similarity in sense of humour, will figure
largely. But we are reliably informed by students of human
interaction that much, perhaps most, of the basis for our judgements about others is unconscious, and it might be that there
are aspects of the complex network of factors underlying our
choices of friends that we are never aware of – even so unexpected a thing as smell or the unrecognised similarity of
appearance, tone of voice, or gesture, of people previously
liked or admired. It is tempting to short-circuit explanations of
why people become friends with each other, especially really

good, close, enduring friends, by putting the words of Montaigne in his essay 'On Friendship' into their mouths: 'If a man urge me to tell wherefore I loved him, I feel it cannot be expressed but by answering: Because it was he, because it was myself.'

Grant that friendship is far more a matter of emotion than rationality, nevertheless in philosophy – 'philosophy' understood in its broadest sense as the mature conversation that humankind has with itself about the things that matter most to it – there has long been discussion about friendship as among the best and most desirable of human relationships. Even if a good many of the examples cited in this tradition of thought are in fact male love relationships, nonetheless these suggest an important fact to be registered: that the ideal of friendship is close to other ideals of human connection, foremost among them love in its own multiplicity of guises and characters. That closeness also invites contrasts; when Oliver Goldsmith said that 'friendship is a disinterested commerce between equals, love an abject intercourse between tyrants and slaves', he said something true about most friendships but only true of some loves, and this reminds us that we are not to expect sharp boundaries in the distinctions we seek to draw, but a field of impressions, of blurred frontiers, where the presence of variety and uniqueness has always to be admitted.

It might be helpful to cast a preliminary eye over the landscape of debate about friendship here; in the main body of the chapters to come only the more central of these themes will be explored in more detail.

No doubt there were thinkers who observed and meditated on human relationships long before classical antiquity. But it is in this latter period that we have the first fully formed engage-ments of intelligence with the subject of friendship and – more completely – the other relationships, principally love, that lie in neighbouring fields. Plato's *Lysis* is the first text we can point to that addresses *philia*, friendship, as distinct from *eros*, passionate love; his *Symposium* is the classic of this latter. But the work that stood for many centuries as the chief point of reference for discussions of friendship was Aristotle's *Nicomachean Ethics*. In a sense it might be said that until modern times everything thought or written about the subject not only did not but could not start anywhere other than with Aristotle.

Aristotle's pre-eminence in the debate arises in large part from the fact that he saw friendship as an essential component of the well-lived and flourishing life, a *eudaimon* life. He argued that the best and highest kind of friendship is that between people who are good, and who each love (*philein*) the other because he – and it is a *he* in this debate – is good. The friend-ship of the good is predicated on virtuous activity, which requires that the parties to it be reflective and capable of the right kind of self-esteem, which enables them to love good others properly. That is a key point: to love another as another self, one must be able to love oneself in the virtuous way (not a selfish, egoistical, conceited way), and this makes one fit to love a virtuous other as identical in interests with oneself. And it was central to Aristotle's conception of the good life that it should consist in pleasant and beneficial activity directed towards friends, which means that the truly good person needs and desires friends so that he can live the good life.

Epicureans and Stoics, perhaps because they lived with more practical needs in more insecure times after the high classical period, had *ataraxia* – tranquillity, peace of mind – as the defining end of a life describable as good. Whereas Epicurus largely agreed with Aristotle's account, he did not, like him, require that friendship can only be the best it can be if it is not instrumental to a further end – that is, if it is an intrinsic good – but held that it is indeed instrumental to the good, namely *ataraxia* itself. Some of the Stoics took a very different view: that the truly Stoical life is one that is indifferent (the desired mental state is *apatheia*) towards what it cannot control, which includes the fate and circumstances of others; and that therefore the fully self-mastered individual will be sufficient to himself and not in need of friends or friendship for the *ataraxia* he seeks to achieve, nor will he mortgage the possibility of achieving *ataraxia* to the fortunes of others' lives, given that he has limited influence over them.

This apparently cold view is not the universal Stoic view; later Stoics were as attached to friends and to friendship as a part of the valuable life – more: to the possibility of living nobly – as one could wish. Their point was not that the imperturbability for which they aimed would exclude the possibility of friendship altogether, but that there is a distinction to be drawn between the normal emotional responses people have towards things, and the 'eupathic' response that is controlled by reason. Emotional reactions never flower into consequences of action or further feeling without the Stoic's reasoned assent. But this allows that eupathic responses can take the form of – be expressed as – friendship or even passionate love: what is distinctively Stoic about them is that they are chosen. The *adaequatio intellectus et rei* – the proper fit between how we think and how things are – is the ground of goodness in life, and 'following nature' (which includes responding to the human instincts for affection, community, and love both in their physical and emotional manifestations) is part of that adequacy.

The work that connected these contributions to the near-thousand years of Christian views on friendship is Cicero's *Laelius: De amicitia*, not least because it was the immediate spur for the thinking not only of Augustine in the fifth century CE but of Aelred of Rievaulx in the twelfth century CE and Thomas Aquinas in the thirteenth century CE. But the importance of Cicero is not confined to its influence: it is a great treatment of the subject in its own right.

There is a feature of Cicero's account, premised as it is on the experience of men of affairs, that is either absent or insufficiently emphasised in the earlier debates: the element of mutual respect, which carries a very important implication: that one recognise that a friend is a different self, not another self as in the Aristotelian idealisation – a point of great significance for anyone whose endeavour to make sense of friendship as it is and should be starts from the thought that a mutual obliteration of identities is not, after all, what ought to be centre-stage in the account we offer.

The idea of friendship was not straightforward for the Christian tradition, in which the ideal of perfect love is the disinterested charitable love known as *agape*. Whereas friendship is individual and preferential, elevating interest in one person over others, thereby privileging the friend in such a way that relationships with others are conditional and of less value, Christian *agape* is intended to be indifferent, universal and unconditional. Augustine – a man of deep friendships – offered this way out: that individual friendship is a divine gift, and a route to the highest love, which is love of the divine. Love for another human is, he argued, instrumental to love of God, but despite being instrumental is elevated and valorised by it. There are echoes of Plato not on *philia* but on the *eros* of the *Symposium* here, in which, likewise, human affection is a path to the transcendent if rightly enacted.

Aelred did not take the same view; he wished to think with Cicero that friendship is its own justification, though with Augustine he wished to think that only Christians could be true friends to each other. His solution was to say that Christian friendship is a spiritual affair, such that friends live in the very heart of charity with one another, enjoying and mutually fostering its constitutive virtues – temperance, prudence, faithfulness, and the like – making friendship an exercise of the godly life.

Aquinas argued that the love of friends – in which one loves another simply and purely for his own sake, and vice versa – is a model for the love of God, in loving whom we make it possible for ourselves to become more like God. It would seem to be implicit in this view that one's relationship with the deity is a superlative form of friendship, which to some suggests this oddity: that on any view, a perfectly self-sufficient being by definition is in need of nothing, including friends and what they might offer to such as need friendship. How then can one be friends with a deity, whose self-sufficiency excludes any basis for reciprocation? For (as Plato has Socrates argue in the *Lysis*) one-sided friendship is scarcely friendship.

Modern views about friendship follow the Renaissance shift of attention from subordinating everything of value to a place in the divine scale, to giving them a place in their own right in the human scale. An evolving thread of difference from and continuity with ancient and medieval views runs from Boccaccio, Montaigne and Bacon through Kant, Emerson, the Utilitarians and Nietzsche to our own contemporary debate. The differences in view are considerable, and increasing.

Kant emphasised community of moral outlook, equality and reciprocity of respect and affection as constitutive of perfect friendship. But these states have to be willed, as a rational act, not founded in emotion, which is non-rational and involuntary because subject to natural law, and which therefore can only at best be instrumental in the establishing of friendship. Furthermore, said Kant, an emotional interest in the happiness of a friend is a barely disguised desire for one's own happiness, given that our attachment to a friend will make us unhappy if for some reason he is unhappy, and therefore in being eager for his happiness we are being eager for our own. Perfect friendship subsists between those who treat each other as 'ends in themselves' irrespective of our own feelings about their welfare.

The contrarian nature of Nietzsche's view – that a friend is one who opposes and thereby strengthens, who challenges, who does not help by lifting part of a friend's burden, but helps him by fighting him – takes the needle to the far side of the dial; Wilde put the matter not much differently in describing a friend as 'one who stabs you in the front'. But even among those still conscious of the classical debate, there is less respect for the ancient pieties – and still less for the pieties of a religion torn between what it sees as differently owed to the sacred and the profane – in the authors who desire more practical and more secular bases for understanding the moral good of friendship. Liberation from the need for a third party in the relationship makes room for a variety of views to emerge. What Montaigne claimed to derive from his friendship with Etienne de La Boétie was a view that out-Aristotles Aristotle in holding that true, perfect, absolute friendship is a complete merging of two selves into one, so that there is no longer even a friendship at issue but an absolute identity beyond explanation: 'because it was him, because it was me'.

Such a response poses a difficulty for utilitarianism, whose principle of maximising happiness or utility for the greatest number shares a problem with Christianity in militating against the preference friends have for one another over non-friends. Can there be a consistent utilitarian view of friendship? Of course there can, in one sense: it maximises utility if everyone is as friendly as possible towards everyone else. Or it might be argued that we maximise overall utility better if each of us concentrates our energies on maximising it for one or more chosen others. But could this be any part of an explanation of what friendship is, why it matters, what motivates us to form friendships and care about our friends?

Views in feminist philosophy pick up the idea of 'caring' – benevolent concern and interest – as crucial, and as trumping the potentially conflicting idea of justice with its connotation of indifferent or equal concern for all others. The mutual relationship of care distinctive of friendship is partial, preferential and voluntary, and its value to the parties is the driver for saying that in a competition between universalist views as embodied in the idea of impartial justice, and the particularism of the 'care perspective', the latter wins. Obviously, though, a distinction needs to be drawn between *friendship* as a theatre of caring and other relationships where a familiar difficulty arises: not all, and perhaps not most, caring relationships are mutual. They are often one-sided, or at least unequal; generalising, one might say that marriage-type relationships between men and women tend to exemplify inequalities of care, and certainly parent–child relationships do. But these are not, or at least not in these forms, friendships – and perhaps it is the inequality that prevents them from being so. If this is right, then it would appear that mutuality in caring and respect for justice are not merely compatible after all, but actually a further constituent in what it is for a relationship to be a form of friendship.

It is almost exclusively in recent discussion that women's perspectives on friendship have been added to the debate. This is a function of the suppression of women's voices in most of history, so that as one looks back across the landscape of interest in this, as with so many other matters, the tone is almost wholly and relentlessly masculine.

In *Testament of Friendship*, her biography of her friend Winifred Holtby, Vera Brittain wrote,

From the days of Homer the friendships of men have enjoyed glory and acclamation, but the friendships of women, in spite of Ruth and Naomi, have usually been not merely unsung, but mocked, belittled and falsely interpreted. I hope that Winifred's story may do something to destroy these tarnished reputations and show its readers that loyalty and affection between women is a noble relationship which far from impoverishing, actually enhances the love of a girl for her lover, of a wife for her husband, of a mother for her children.[1]

What is surprising now about these remarks is their apologetic character; even here 'loyalty and affection between women' is not allowed to stand in its own right but requires justification in terms of the lover, husband or children who have prior claim on that loyalty and affection.

The obvious reason is that until very recently it has been nigh impossible for women to be defined otherwise than in connection with the roles that women play – as girlfriends, wives and mothers, nurses, teachers of the young. Brittain quotes May Sinclair's introduction to an edition of Mrs Gaskell's *Life of Charlotte Brontë*:

> By suppressing Haworth churchyard and Charlotte Brontë's relations, it would be possible to write a 'Life' of her which would be all gaiety and sunshine. The lives of great men admit of these suppressions. Their relations on the whole do not affect them except as temporary obstacles (more or less offensive) to their career . . .
>
> It is otherwise with great women. They cannot thus get rid of their relations. Their lives are inseparable from them, their work in many cases inexplicable without them . . . A woman cannot get away from her family even in its absence. She may abandon it; it may abandon her; but she is bound to it by infrangible indestructible bonds. It, and all it has done to her or for her, has an enduring life in her memory. However much abandoned or ignored, its persistence there endows it with immortality. Imagine then what its influence must have been on Charlotte, who never abandoned or ignored it.[2]

And yet – to generalise – the attestation of anecdote and experience is that friendships between women can be and often are closer, more enduring, more confidential and supportive, more intimate, more powerful and complete, than is customary among men, whose companionships are often predicated on doing things together rather than saying things to each other, masking taciturnities about private and intimate matters with attachments instead to external matters – to careers, sports, news, practical interests, and the like.

Some of the foregoing paragraphs offer a sketch of the conceptual terrain and, as noted, only some of the more central themes and features mentioned will be explored in the following pages. But it is important to note that it is not in philosophy as such – the discursive enterprise of conceptual analysis – but in literature that one finds a more minute inspection of friendship as lived rather than as a concept, an abstraction, an idealisation, and a subject for theorising. It cannot for example be merely coincidence that Plato and Aristotle discussed friendship against the background of a public conversation in which Sophocles and Aeschylus were dominant voices, and where *philoi* – those in the bond of *philia* – were family and kin too, not just chosen others. If the natural ties of kinship were taken to apply in the chosen ties of friendship, and if these could be extended to foreigners too – *xenoi* – then we have an interest in knowing what commonalities link them.

At some point it is necessary to look at the examples of friendship given to us by literary and legendary tradition to see what the models were in the minds of those who theorised; I do so in a chapter which divides the historical survey of ideas about friendship from the discussion I give of how in our contemporary setting we might view its variety and complexity, and its centrality to the good and flourishing life.

Note that this is not a history of friendship, not a sociological or a psychological treatise on friendship, not a self-help or New Age manual about friendship; rather, it is a discussion of the *idea* of friendship, a philosophical (in the broadest sense) exploration of views about it.

In Part I, I survey discussions of friendship mainly in the history of philosophy, beginning with the classic sources that have shaped so much of subsequent thinking on the topic. Part II is an excursus into the examples in legend and literature of great friendships, so often cited by those who examine the subject, and which we must therefore know about too. Part III addresses contemporary debates about friendship, and offers my own views and experiences in response to the foregoing. For this last, the justification is that in the end the personal and the subjective are the ultimate measures of what we find plausible in this field – making it one of the few fields where this is legitimately so, and all the more significant for being so.

I range widely through philosophical, historical and literary sources for my materials, not methodically and systematically, but as occasion and need suggest. As when sinking one's instruments into ocean currents at various places, one eventually gets a sense of their drift: that has been part of the technique here.

PART I

Ideas

CHAPTER 1

The *Lysis* and *Symposium*

Friendships existed long before anyone thought to analyse them, and even longer again before anyone thought to write philosophical treatises about them. But when the first serious discussions of friendship appeared – and it is no surprise that they did so in that fountainhead of Western civilisation, the classical period of antiquity in Greece – they laid the ground for almost all the debate that followed.

As the first philosophical text directly to address the concept of friendship, Plato's dialogue *Lysis* has to stand at the head of the discussion. It must be introduced with a caveat, however; which is that it is a somewhat unsatisfying treatment, and not only for the reason common to much of Plato's earlier work, which is that it is inconclusive and leaves its subject in as much unclarity as it began, but also because it exemplifies too fully a characteristic of those dialogues: the sophistries which allow Socrates his too-easy victories over his interlocutors, who ought not to let him get away with them.

These reservations apart, there are two useful features of the *Lysis* discussion. One consists in the throwaway comments on friendship that Socrates and his interlocutors accept as truisms, illustrating what Greeks of their time thought about the matter. The other is the contrast between these truisms – along with the other points about friendship made in the *Lysis* – and the concepts of love discussed in Plato's more famous dialogue, the *Symposium*.

The commonplaces about friendship which Plato assumes in the *Lysis* were not accepted in their entirety by Aristotle, whose own much fuller and more detailed discussion of friendship in the *Nicomachean Ethics* is in part a reaction to the *Lysis* view, most especially in rejecting its casual commitment to friendship having a utilitarian aspect as part of its very essence – that is, as turning on the usefulness of friends to each other, or (which in Aristotle's view is worse) of one of them to the other.

The contrast between friendship in Plato's *Lysis* and love in his *Symposium* is intriguing, not least because the *Lysis* discussion proceeds as if the concept of one kind of love – that of an older male for a younger – at least largely overlaps with the concept of friendship, even though, as the dialogue acknowledges in passing, the latter is more extensive. The *Symposium* is a later and philosophically far more achieved work whose aim is very different: it serves the purpose of establishing that love of the Form of Beauty is an integral part of what constitutes the good life, an overarching ethical claim absent from the *Lysis* despite its (again passing) allusions to virtues and other non-virtue desiderata. In the *Symposium* the concept of friendship – *philia*, the subject of the *Lysis* – is subordinate to the *eros* discussed in the *Symposium*, and whose eventual refinement into 'Platonic love' is described to Socrates by (so he tells his companions) a priestess of Mantinea called Diotima.

The *Lysis* is ostensibly narrated by Socrates himself. He recounts being stopped one day by a group of boys as he walked back into Athens from the Academy, and being invited by them to join their talk. He asks one of them, a youth called Hippothales, if he has a 'favourite' – meaning, someone he is in love with – and is told that Hippothales' favourite is a boy named Lysis, son of a wealthy and patrician citizen called Democrates. We are to imagine that Hippothales is in his mid-teens, Lysis about twelve, which makes the pair much younger than is normally the case for relationships of the connoted kind. This is doubtless deliberate, because the dialogue is more concerned with the relationship between Lysis and a boy of his own age, Menexenus, which is straightforwardly a friendship and has no erotic overtones, thus contrasting it with the passion felt by Hippothales for Lysis, which we are given to understand is not requited.

It is accordingly a bit of byplay in which Socrates tells Hippothales that he is wooing Lysis in entirely the wrong way, by praising him and his family, writing poetry and songs in Lysis' honour, and singing them to him. Instead, says Socrates, Hippothales should remind Lysis that he is still an ignorant child, thus putting him down rather than buttering him up: 'That is the way, Hippothales, in which you should talk to your beloved, humbling and lowering him, and not as you do, puffing him up and spoiling him.'[1]

The meat of the discussion of friendship occurs not in this demonstration itself but in its framing. Socrates asks Lysis' friend Menexenus which of the two of them is older.

'That is a matter of dispute between us,' he said.

'And which is the nobler? Is that also a matter of dispute?'

'Yes, certainly.'

'And do you also dispute which is the more beautiful?'

The two boys laughed.

'I shall not ask which is the richer of the two,' I said; 'for you are friends, are you not?'

'Certainly,' they replied.

'And friends have all things in common, so that one of you can be no richer than the other, if you say truly that you are friends.'

They assented. I was about to ask which was the juster and which the wiser of the two; but at this moment Menexenus was called away . . .[2]

Justice, wisdom and nobility are virtues, beauty – physical beauty – and wealth are not; in quizzing the boys Socrates is exploring the question that, on the evidence of the *Charmides*, he always liked to have answered: whether this or that notable youth has the characteristic which is greater than physical beauty, namely, nobility of soul.[3] Of interest to us is the throw-away remark, ' "I shall not ask which is the richer of the two," I said; "for you are friends, are you not? . . . And friends have all things in common, so that one of you can be no richer than the other, if you say truly that you are friends".'

The next assumption appears near the end of Socrates' 'lowering and humbling' attack on Lysis, where he asks him, ' ". . . shall we be friends to others, and will any others love us, in matters where we are useless to them? . . . And therefore my boy, if you become wise, all men will be your friends and kindred, for you will be useful and good; but if you are not wise, neither father, nor mother, nor kindred, nor anyone else, will be your friends." '4

We thus learn that friends are those who hold all things in common, and are useful to each other. This is the picture we have in mind when we read Socrates' passionate asseveration that the one thing he has always, with all his heart, longed for more than anything else, is friends: ' "I must tell you that I am one who from my childhood upward have set my heart upon a certain possession . . . I have a passion for friends . . . Yea, by the dog of Egypt, I should greatly prefer a real friend to all the gold of Darius . . ."'5 He tells Menexenus how he envies the perfect friendship that he and Lysis seem so easily to have established, and wishes to quiz him on how they managed it. But then the dialogue collapses into a sophistical exercise of tying Menexenus in knots over whether a pair can be mutual friends if only one loves the other, and how one can determine in that case which is the friend, for if the friend is he who loves another then it might turn out that people can be loved by their enemies, who are therefore their friends . . . and so on into paradox.6

This part of the discussion might have been short-circuited by Menexenus if he had refused to accept that there can be true friendship which is not mutual, and that although one person can unrequitedly love (the dialogue still speaks of *philia* not *eros*) another and therefore be a friend to him, the relationship itself would need to be qualified accordingly; for whatever it is, it does not deserve the name of friendship as such.

More to the point is the discussion in which Socrates and Lysis agree that there is something to the idea that like attracts but that since evil men are like each other but might well be good friends to each other because of their evilness, friendship should only be seen as the mutuality of good people who are alike. But Socrates slides from this to the generalisation that 'the good are friends' (permitted by the idea that those who are alike in being good are otherwise alike: a fallacy) and then declares that he is not satisfied with it[7] – as indeed he should not be, for those who are alike in some respects might be very different in other respects, and their being alike in goodness might be the only respect in which they are alike. His reason is that if two people are alike, they can only get from one another what they can get from themselves: 'And if neither can be of any use to the other, how can they feel affection for one another?' Since Lysis feebly agrees both to this sophistical reasoning and to the instrumental view of friendship it supports, Socrates is able to conclude that 'the like is not the friend of the like in so far as he is like',[8] thus apparently denying what we instinctively know to be true, namely, that shared interests and outlook, a similar sense of humour and a shared past make potent cement in relationships, and is surely what we mean in talking of people being 'like' one another.

Socrates then finds a way of refuting the thought that 'the good may be the friend of the good in so far as he is good' by arguing that because good people, in virtue of being so, are self-sufficient and have no need of anyone else, and because 'he who wants nothing will feel affection for nothing . . . and he who loves not is not a lover or a friend', it follows that the good will not be the friend of the good.[9] This is a classic example of early Platonic sophistry ('the good are self-sufficient, therefore they lack nothing, therefore they will feel no affection for anything'; these transitions are obviously spurious).

And so the argument proceeds, with Socrates considering whether opposites are most likely to establish friendships, and the degree to which friendship is a matter of need ('medicine is a friend to health' because sickness needs medicine), and whether it is congeniality that makes for friendship – though he acknowledges that the distinction between congeniality and likeness is unclear. 'If neither the beloved, nor the lover, nor the like, nor the unlike, nor the good, nor the congenial, nor any other of whom we spoke – for there were such a number of them that I cannot remember all – if none of these are friends, I know not what remains to be said.'[10] And at that point the bodyguards of the boys arrive to take them home, leaving the discussion in an unfinished state. That it is left in such a state is no surprise; it was not moving towards a conclusion anyway.

Nevertheless, Plato appears to be sure about two things in the *Lysis*. One is that mutual utility is a founding principle of friendship, and the other is that in the catechising of Menexenus early in the dialogue he has Socrates make it clear that the usefulness of an individual to another, and to his family and community, is a condition of his being regarded as a friend both to him and to them. The unremarked slippage from the personal to the social – it equivocates to treat 'friend' in 'friend to his community' and 'friend to Lysis' – does not however affect the point that, for Plato, mutual utility underlies friendship and is constitutive of its very nature. This is the point with which Aristotle so trenchantly disagreed.

An oddity in the account is how much Plato under-appreciates the persuasiveness of the 'congeniality' point, which we in our modern understanding of friendship take for granted as essential. He is right to be troubled about whether there is much difference between congeniality and likeness, though he should be more troubled by the spurious argument that if two people are alike they can find no use in each other. On the contrary, mutual reinforcement of attitudes and the easiness which arises from sharing beliefs, practices and tastes is taken to be a profound reason for friendship, and would undoubtedly have been as obvious a source of bonding between Lysis and Menexenus as any other.

Indeed the assumption that friends will, if true friends, share their wealth in common says that sharing things other than wealth – confidences, opportunities, interests, tastes – is likewise a principle of friendship.

And there is the datum that whatever complex of reasons can be adduced for people liking one another, the simple truth is that people can and do take a liking to each other: and that this can be enough to start a friendship, even if it is in the end not enough to sustain it. So when Socrates says what he does at the end, he should have taken a hint from it: 'O Menexenus and Lysis, how ridiculous that you two boys, and I, as an old man, who venture to range myself with you, should imagine ourselves to be friends – this is what the bystanders will go away and say – and as yet we have not been able to discover what is a friend!'[11]

Obviously enough, Lysis, Menexenus and Socrates would not be described by bystanders as lovers of one another. The sentiment they share is *philia*, not *eros*. The *Lysis*'s exploration of *philia* stands at a considerable remove from the terminus of the *Symposium*'s discussion of love. At one point in the *Lysis* there is a possible hint of things to come, where Socrates gets his young interlocutors to agree that friendship is caused by desire, and desire is for something lacked by the desirer, and that what is lacked and is therefore dear to the desirer is what is congenial to him.[12] This result is a declension from where the argument seems to be going at first, namely, that the sentiments constitutive of friendship are in fact intimations of a desire for, and a lack of, congress in body or mind with something that the immediate object of those sentiments merely represents – something metaphysically higher. In the *Symposium* we meet this thought in full. There we learn that love in the more exigent sense of *eros* is desire for what lies beyond and above all the instances or instantiations of what is desired, which in the sublunary sense is the beauty of the beloved: and this far further thing is the Form of Beauty itself.

The *Symposium* is a great piece of art, and its serious metaphysical aspect is only part of a work whose geniality and good humour are a window into the Athens we know as the cradle of our thought. We see Socrates at a drinking party hosted by the dramatist Agathon, along with a number of other distinguished guests, and it ends after the late drunken arrival of Alcibiades, the celebrated but controversial statesman and soldier who loved Socrates and claimed to have made several unsuccessful attempts on his virtue. When he gatecrashes Agathon's party near the end of the *Symposium* he gives an amusing account of crawling into Socrates' bed only to be rebuffed.

The opening speeches by Phaedrus and Agathon are admirable for their literary qualities, but do not contribute much to the question of the nature of love. After Phaedrus' literary allusions to that noble aspect of *eros* which makes the lover lay down his life for his beloved – he cites Achilles and Patroclus – we have Pausanias describing the situation in contemporary Athens in which it is accepted that men will love boys, but that boys must be guarded from the attentions of men, a double standard that Pausanias decries on the grounds that if the man's attitude is honourable and his aim is to educate his beloved in prudence and wisdom, the relationship ought to be encouraged. This is a higher form of love than the 'vulgar' love which has its focus on physical satisfaction. It is implicit in the tale that two of those present at the party, Eryximachus and Phaedrus, had begun their long-standing relationship in just that way.

In contrasting ways Eryximachus and Aristophanes reprise the familiar ideas that love arises between opposites or between incomplete halves. In replying to Agathon's poetic invocation of love as a juvenile deity, Socrates rejects the idea that love can be divine, for it involves desire, and desire is for what one lacks, and therefore the love is not felt by one who is rich or wise, but by one who seeks wealth and wisdom. A person who is aware of being ignorant strives for wisdom, unlike either the god who is already wise or the foolish person who is unaware of being ignorant.

And then Socrates claims to be rehearsing what he learned from the priestess Diotima: that the beauty represented in an individual – for example in the body of a beautiful youth – is an instance of what is present in the beauty of bodies in general, and which makes them beautiful. Realisation of this leads on to thoughts of the beauty of minds, and thence of moral nobility and knowledge, and by these gradations finally to Beauty itself, the imperishable, perfect and eternal Form of Beauty.

In this account love – *eros* – is desire for everything good, if the greatest goods, among them beauty, happiness and truth, are truly separable. The familiar physical passions of *eros* are merely the first intimation of desire, and because desire is innate and has the potential to be elevated in its aim to higher and eventually the highest form – that is, the metaphysical Form – of its objects, this shows that we are by nature predisposed to seek the good. The obverse of this coin is that desire is awareness of deficit, of what we lack; that is the thrust of Socrates' reply to Agathon. But the positive implication of this is that the quest of the ultimate good is founded on self-knowledge, which involves a recognition of deficiency, and a determination to remedy it. In Diotima's lecture to Socrates the point is made that just as sexual desire has procreation as its aim, so desire for the ultimate good has a higher procreation as an aim: the generating, nurturing and passing on of wisdom.

Neither in the account of more prosaic love in the *Symposium*, nor in the metaphysical version of its highest expression, is there any consideration of friendship. From the point of view of *eros* conceived in such a way as to make it the gradient to the highest of moral and intellectual aspirations, *philia* seems prosaic and minor. It is certainly different, even if it were neither of these more reductive things.[13]

There is a loftiness of thought in the *Symposium*'s final idealised view of love that makes it appear great; but it is an unrealistic view nonetheless. It asks us to think that the encounter with everything attractive and lovable will, if we are reflective, make us move beyond the physical to a purely intellectual contemplation of abstractions. 'Platonic love' is ethereal, unphysical, denatured love. The common and healthy desire felt by people who love each other to hug, kiss, touch, make love, and thereby gain the satisfactions and completions of physical and through it psychological intimacy, recoils from the idea of a fastidiously abstract state which, in being exclusively intellectual is unexpressible in any way other than by the largest and finest-sounding words. This does not connect with the reality either of love or friendship, and does not begin to touch the connections between them. And this is because it is about relationships not between people, but between minds and the abstract ideas they contemplate.

When people think of the first truly classic statement of a view about friendship, therefore, it is not to Plato they turn, but to his great pupil and successor, Aristotle.

CHAPTER 2

The Classic Statement: Aristotle

The word *philia* is made to do express duty for the sentiment of friendship in Plato's *Lysis*, but it also – as noted in passing in the Introduction – meant much more, embracing family ties and even socio-political ones. Plato's usage seems to have secured it to friendship for the philosophical debate, however, for in the eighth and ninth books of the *Nicomachean Ethics* it is *philia* – and along with it an identification of the qualities that attract people into friendship with each other, 'lovables' or *phileta* – which is used to denote the sentiment of friendship. But in passing Aristotle applies it in the conventional way not just to family members but to travellers from foreign parts, and says that it exists even among the birds and beasts.[1] Convergence in attitudes and aims of the kind that keeps cities together 'seems to be similar, in a way, to friendship', he says, which is why political action is aimed at achieving it.[2]

This was no idle remark. The *Nicomachean Ethics* precedes the *Politics* for good reason. 'Society depends on friendship,'

Aristotle says there; 'after all, people will not even take a journey in common with their enemies.'[3] He says '*philia* is the motive of society',[4] and that it is even more important than justice because it is what promotes concord in the city.[5]

Aristotle describes friendship as an 'excellence', and essential to the living of a good and worthwhile life. Even those – indeed, perhaps especially those – who have wealth or power need friends, he says, for how otherwise would they be able to show beneficence, or protect their wealth and position, which are more at risk the greater they are? Moreover, 'in poverty and all other kinds of misfortune people think of their friends as their only refuge'.[6] And friends help each other; they help the young to learn, they care for the old, and encourage those in their prime to behave finely.

So far these remarks imply that friendship is useful and, correlatively, an acknowledgement of deficiencies in need of being supplied. But although these commonplaces are true, they do not get to the nub of the matter. What is the nature of the friendship that serves these purposes, and are these purposes all that there is to friendship? And what is or could be the highest, best or most distinctive aspect of it? Aristotle mentions the 'disputes' that arise in efforts to answer these questions, with some saying that friendship is a matter of like attracting like, while others argue that it arises in the mutual attraction of opposites – both of them familiar and conventional views in competition with each other, and which Aristotle's own succinct definition – 'a man becomes a friend when he is loved and returns that love and this is recognised by both men in question' – by itself leaves open.[7] To clarify matters, Aristotle says, we should instead begin by asking 'what is it that is loved?' What are the *phileta* or 'lovables'?

There are three *phileta*, he says, and they are what is useful, what is pleasing, and what is excellent. These correlate to three kinds of friends: those who are friends with each other because of the advantages gained by being so, those who are friends with each other because of the pleasure it brings them to be so, and those who are friends with each other because they 'resemble each other in excellence' and love each other because of 'what the other *is*'.[8] This last, he says, is the truest and highest kind of friendship.

The friendships of utility and pleasure are incidental affairs, easily ended when the utility or pleasure evaporates, as in their nature they are all too prone to do.[9] This is clear in the case of the pleasure-based friendships of the young, who live by emotion and seek immediate gratification in what lies close to hand; and they are erotically inclined, says Aristotle, which adds to the propensity for quick beginnings and endings, especially in those youthful friendships.[10]

Friendship between virtuous people – people who are good without qualification; good in themselves – is lasting and complete. Utility and pleasure are comprehended in this friendship, but they are not constitutive of it; its constitutive aspects lie in the fact that it is the friendship of people who are alike in virtue, and who wish good things for each other both because these things are good in themselves and because each is recognised by the other as good in himself. The friendship between them 'lasts so long as they are good, and excellence is something lasting'.[11] Desiring the good for the other is *eunoia*, 'goodwill' (the English term 'benevolence' derives from the Latin cognate).

A problem implicit in the nature of friendship thus conceived, from Aristotle's own point of view, is that it is not going to be achieved by many, for there are too few people with a sufficient degree of virtue and *eunoia* to make it general.[12] At one point, indeed, Aristotle seems to think that his account offers such an idealised and demanding portrait of friendship that it could never be realised in practice: 'Friends! there is no friend!' he despairingly says. If it were thought that goodwill is sufficient for friendship, not merely necessary, the problem would be resolved; but goodwill is not itself friendship, since people can have good will towards those who are not friends; rather, it is the starting point of friendship and, as with like-mindedness, a concomitant of it.[13]

Aristotle famously then says that '[a person] is to his friend as he is to himself, for his friend is another self'.[14] We can therefore read off the attributes of friendship from the concern that an individual has for himself. The self-respecting person

wishes for what is good for himself, and what appears good, and he does it (for it is a mark of a good person to work hard at what is good), and for his own sake (he does it for the sake of the thinking element of himself, which is what each of us is thought to be). He also wishes himself to live and be kept safe, and most of all that with which he understands, since to the good person existing is something good, and each of us wishes good things for himself.[15]

The typical features of friendship derived from these ways that people relate to themselves include, he says, the following: we wish good to ourselves, to be safe, to spend time with ourselves, to have pleasant memories, to have good hopes for the future, to have materials for thoughtful reflection, and to 'share his grief and his pleasures with himself'.[16] Because a friend is another self, we wish all these things for him too.

Much is made of the 'another self' claim in subsequent treatments of friendship, and indeed most of the discussions, all the way to Montaigne, appear to concentrate on this remark above all the other things Aristotle says in a long and complex discussion of the varieties of friendship and why the friendship of virtuous equals is best. Yet the remark is almost parenthetical, and the context of discussion has as much to do with the appropriateness of proper self-love as it does with defining the meaning of 'friend'. In my view the overemphasis on Aristotle's 'another self' phrase in all the subsequent history of discussion about friendship has been the single most distorting aspect in our understanding of it, for the very good reason that it has to be part of the voluntary obligations attached to being a good friend to accept the differences between oneself and one's friend – which involves giving one's friend space to have some interests and tastes different from one's own, and to agree to disagree about some things.

The point about self-love is a significant one, for it is obvious that if the highest form of friendship is mutuality between people of excellent character, then the self-cultivation and self-mastery required for excellence of character require, just as they lead to, self-respect. When both parties to a friendship have this attitude to themselves, and regard the other as entitled to the same consideration as they give themselves, then the relationship is, as it should be, complete.

The point is therefore no different, except in expression, from saying that a real friend is one who feels what she does for her friend for her friend's own sake. She does not like or love her because of what she can get from the relationship or because it happens for the time being to be enjoyable; these are the incomplete or imperfect friendships which are not destined to last. Reciprocity is another feature: true friends think and feel the same way about each other, something made possible by the fact that their relationships are based on virtue – each party to the relationship is a virtuous person, and each recognises and loves this fact about the other. And this is further to say that the best kind of friendship is based on character, and moreover the best kind of character, which is the reason – in Aristotle's view – for its relative rarity.

As mentioned, Aristotle does not restrict the use of 'friendship' to denote only those relationships where mutual benevolence felt for the other's intrinsic sake is its basis, because he is practical enough to recognise that relationships based on utility and pleasure are types of friendship too, just as are kin relations and amicable transactions with foreigners. But they are not 'complete' – that is the point; and in not being so, they are far less likely to endure, and are of lower intrinsic value.

Recall that Aristotle thinks that friendship is an essential constituent of the good life and the happiness that characterises it – *eudaimonia*. The question therefore arises whether only the highest kind of friendship is such a constituent, or can the incomplete kinds also serve? It is clear from Aristotle's opening discussion about how we need friends in order to exercise our beneficence and secure help in times of need that friendship as such, not necessarily or only the highest form of it, is a desideratum.

The characteristic streak of pragmatism in Aristotle is at work here. Earlier in the *Nicomachean Ethics* he remarks that making a contribution to society is of as much importance to being virtuous as anything we do or achieve in the private realm: at one point he says it is finer to benefit the city at large than to make one other person happy.[17] This thought does not quite contradict, but nevertheless sits at an angle to, the idea that friendship is 'necessary to life' for the reasons given at the outset of his discussion of the subject. But because the quest of the good is an overriding one, it would surely seem that anything that conduces to *eudaimonia* has equal value to anything else thus conducive. The resounding claim at the outset of Aristotle's writing on ethics is that the good is that at which all things aim, the thing which is intrinsically desirable and to which all other positive things aim.[18] If friendship is integral to the good life, and the good is the ultimate aim, then friendship – an individual and private thing – has at least as great a significance as civic contribution; and that really does seem to resist the claim that it is 'finer and more godlike' to advance the interests of one's city than to make another person happy.

The point can be differently made. By *eudaimonia* Aristotle meant an activity, not a state or quality. In the first book of the *Nicomachean Ethics* he defines it as 'the activity of the mind deriving from virtue,' remembering that 'virtue' means 'excellence'.[19] The activity in question is what expresses and fulfils the highest and most distinctive attribute of human beings, which is their capacity to be rational. Rationality enables them to work out what the courageous, temperate, generous, modest or (generally) right thing is to do in a given circumstance, by identifying the middle course between extremes constituting the vices opposite to those virtues: for example, rashness or cowardice on either side of courage, meanness or profligacy on either side of generosity. The development and application of practical wisdom – *phronesis* – enable one to steer that middle path, thus to be virtuous, and thus to live a life of *eudaimonia*.

But for all that Aristotle's pragmatism and common sense are here fully on display, this view does not represent the terminus of his case. In the first pages of the *Nicomachean Ethics* he identifies three kinds of life: the life of pleasure, the life of virtuous activity on behalf of one's community (the political life), and the contemplative philosophical life, devoted to grasping the ultimate nature of things.[20] From what he says of the highest and most distinctive thing about human beings, namely their possession of rationality, one can readily infer which of these lives is in his view best, and which therefore is most fully eudaimonic. And although such a life might be enhanced by having friends with whom to exchange ideas about supreme and final questions, the clear implication is that philosophical contemplation is a solitary and detached activity.

The observation that the best is the enemy of the good might seem to apply rather squarely to Aristotle's account. He is surely right to say that a life without friends would, at very least, be an impoverished one, and for the reasons that he begins by noting: that without friends we have no field for the exercise of beneficence, no helpers and supporters in times of need, no bond that keeps communities together, no teachers of the young or carers of the old, no encouragers to virtue for those in the prime of life. Yet there is more to the matter: if friendly sentiments can be felt towards strangers as well as kin, and if even animals can be friends to their own kind, then friendship has a strong claim to being essential *simpliciter*, not 'essential for' something else – intrinsic as a value, not instrumental. This is expressly what Aristotle's best kind of friendship is intended to be.

However, although this view is consistent with the idea that there are 'lower' forms of friendship predicated on mutual pleasure or usefulness, a question arises whether the fact that a friend is a 'good in itself' for the other friend (this being mutual) is consistent with the 'good for oneself' of loving that friend. Since the latter is instrumental in conducing to one's own good, it is inconsistent with the austere conception of treating the other as a good in himself without any instrumental benefit to oneself. Is this a problem? It would be the most strained kind of purism to argue that the best kind of friendship *must* be such that its defining features are irrelevant to the welfare of the parties to it considered individually, not least because this would require us to regard a friendship as an independently existing abstraction. But as an important component of the good life it is, obviously, good for the friend that he is a friend, not merely in being the object of the disinterested love of his friend, but in himself loving his friend disinterestedly likewise. If the relationship is mutual, each party is both an agent and a patient of the process; so there can be no inconsistency between treating the other as a good in himself and one's loving him as a good for oneself as well as him.

There is room in Aristotle's conception of *eudaimonia* for regarding the activity of being a friend not merely as a conductor to the highest good but as part of what is constitutive of the highest good. That is surely what 'being essential' is. But if so there is a different tension in Aristotle's view, one that serves as a ground for rejecting the idea that contemplation is exclusively the highest good. If *eudaimonia* is an activity, and if the highest quality of such activity consists in solitary contemplation of ultimate things, friendship would not be essential to it; but friendship is essential to the good life. Aristotle cannot have it both ways. The 'solitary contemplation of the highest good' is reminiscent of the impractical ideality of Plato's views, with which Aristotle's more pragmatic temper is so often at odds. Here therefore we see a residue of Plato's influence on his former pupil, creating an inconsistency.

But the active sense of friendship as an essential feature of *eudaimonia* seems to me to trump Aristotle's add-on view of the highest good as the solitary contemplation of abstractions. Moreover if we were to accept his own view that promoting concord in the city is a 'finer and more godlike thing' than personal friendship, then given that this is an even more practical and social activity, yet further removed from the anchoritic distance of contemplation, we see that the tension between these two aspects of his view is unsustainable.

Aristotle's immediate successors in the debate were unsurprisingly more taken by the significance of the personal bond than any suggestion of its subordination to a putatively higher ethereal end, for after all the realities and practicalities of life make friendship a down-to-earth business, with laughter and food and wine, and activities like helping each other move furniture when necessary, as ordinary accompaniments. It was the Christian thinkers who reverted to a more ethereal aspect of the view, for like Aristotle in his metaphysical mood they had transcendental fish to fry.

In fastening on Aristotle's 'another self' remark as his defining view of what is meant by 'friend', almost all later contributors to the discussion found themselves in considerable agreement about the nature of friendship. As already noted, this in my view is a mistake. But Aristotle himself was not as wedded to the 'another self' notion as his successors made him seem. The idea of seeing friendship as a relationship in important part predicated on wishing the good, and promoting the good, for one's friend, and of this itself contributing to the good of one's own life, is surely part of what we have to mean by friendship, and although it seems, once it is explicitly stated, an obvious enough insight, it is too central to be treated as merely implicit.

CHAPTER 3

Cicero *De amicitia*

There is a good reason why Erasmus and Hume, among many others, valued Cicero – and for more reasons than the famous beauty of his prose. It is that certain of his treatises are as valuable in content as in style. It is true that much of his philosophical writing is, as his critics say, derivative and superficial; but the essays 'On Old Age' (*Cato Maior De senectute*) and 'Laelius: On Friendship' (*Laelius: De amicitia*), and especially this last, belong in the first rank of discussions of their subject matter.

The chapters on friendship in Aristotle's *Nicomachean Ethics* are careful explorations of the kind especially approved by philosophers in the analytic tradition today, for whom the painstaking business of conceptual clarification and the drawing of fine distinctions are the essence of their craft. Although most of his strictures are directed at Stoics, Epicureans and others whose views he disagreed with, Cicero might have had Aristotle in mind when he wrote of his own approach, which was that he does not go into the subject of friendship in the same manner as those who discuss it 'with more than usual accuracy, and it may be correctly, but with too little view to practical results'.[1] 'Practical results' – the actuality, reality and pragmatics of friendship – are what interested him, and his account of them in the *De amicitia* is in consequence richly human. Even though it draws on Aristotle and other sources, in its breadth of view it is arguably the best classical discussion extant. It carries the weight of Cicero's experience as a public man, and the plausibility of real historical examples which his contemporary readers knew and could judge.

Cicero sided with Pompey against Caesar in the civil wars that effectively ended the Roman Republic, so after Pompey's defeat, and Caesar's pardon of him in acknowledgement of his former great services to Rome, Cicero withdrew from public life. In the quiet of his country retreat he devoted himself to writing, and in less than three years, 46 to 44 BCE, produced an extraordinary list of works, among them his best. It was not only despair at the demise of the Republic that drove him to seek solace in work, but the even profounder grief caused by the death of his only daughter, whom he greatly loved.

In brief intervals in the three decades of public life preceding this, Cicero had continued the avid study of philosophy that he began in his youth. Its fruits appear in these works. He was not an original thinker, but a skilful organiser of ideas, which he expressed with marvellous clarity and elegance. It would, by the way, be wrong to infer a demotion of him because of that phrase 'not an original thinker', for after all very few people are so. In the judgement of more recent intellectual history hardly anyone comes close to Plato and Aristotle in this league. Yet it takes great powers to do what Cicero did, which was to understand, arrange and articulate important ideas well, and when one considers the fact that his works are in print two thousand years after their composition, and that he has always been admired by excellent judges for the best of what he did, it would be a mistake to devalue his achievement because of that comparison, which is yet another instance of the harm that the best does to the good.

Although the influence of Aristotle's thought is obvious in *De amicitia*, it is not the only and perhaps not the chief source of its ideas. Cicero makes direct use of material from Xenophon's *Memorabilia* also, words there attributed to Socrates being here given to Scipio; and both Diogenes Laertius and Aulus Gellius state that Cicero's principal source was a now-lost three-volume work on friendship by Theophrastus. Students of Cicero's work take the view that although the influences are identifiable, and indeed Cicero references them at times, it is clear that, as his Loeb translator William Falconer says, the 'arrangement, plan, style and illustrations are his own. Certainly no other author of ancient or modern times has discussed the subject of friendship with so much completeness and charm as Cicero.'[2]

As a youth Cicero studied law with the augur Quintus Mucius Scaevola, a learned man and son-in-law of the Gaius Laelius who is the main speaker in *De amicitia*. Laelius is represented as being asked by Scaevola and another son-in-law, Gaius Fannius, to talk about friendship because of his famous lifelong bond with Scipio Amaelianus. Cicero set the dialogue shortly after Scipio's death in 129 BCE, when Laelius was freshly grieving for his lost friend. It is surmised that Cicero had himself heard of Laelius' account from Scaevola when he became his student in 90 BCE. Nearly eighty years separate the date of writing from the dramatic date, and nearly fifty years from the time Cicero first heard Scaevola speak of what Laelius had to say on the subject of his friendship with Scipio. Obviously, Cicero is using whatever he heard from Scaevola merely as a hook, but there is no doubt that an attitude and some details deriving from that almost legendary friendship lie near the centre of Cicero's account.

Laelius and Scipio fought together in the Iberian campaigns of 210–206 BCE, during which Laelius' victories in charge of the Roman fleet in the attack on New Carthage, and at the head of the cavalry at the battle of Zama, made significant contributions to Scipio's overall victory. According to the historian Polybius, to whom Laelius in old age gave much information about Scipio and his campaigns, the two men were friends from childhood, though Laelius was of lower social status from a less rich family. After their military adventures they held office together in the Roman state, helping each other in different ways, but with Laelius always the junior – a fact that made no difference to the friendship between them.

Just how close and enduring a friendship it was is clear from Laelius' remarks on the grief he felt in losing Scipio.

Without affection and goodwill life can hold no joys. Scipio was suddenly snatched away . . . We shared the same house, ate the same meals side by side; we were soldiers together, together we travelled, together we went on our holidays in the countryside. We devoted every minute of our spare time together to study and learning, hidden from the world but enjoying each other's company.[3]

Laelius' disquisition on friendship is offered as the practical reflections of a mature and experienced mind, not as those of an abstruse philosopher. He begins by saying that there is nothing greater in the world than friendship, for it fits human nature, and is exactly what people both need and desire in all experiences of life. But he makes a conventional stipulation: 'I must at the very beginning lay down this principle: that true friendship can only exist between good people'[4] – meaning by 'good people' those whom we recognise as such, using our practical common sense rather than the refinements of 'pedantic accuracy'. A good person, on a practical understanding of the term, is one who is honourable, just, generous, courageous and loyal, and free from greed, intemperance and violence.[5]

Laelius' account then proceeds as follows. There is a natural propensity to prefer kin to fellow citizens, and these to strangers; that is just a fact. But what is obvious is that the difference between friendship and mere acquaintanceship is the goodwill (*benevolentia*; perhaps 'affection' captures the sense better) distinctive of the former. Eliminate goodwill from acquaintanceship and it still exists in name; eliminate it from a friendship, and that friendship no longer exists as friendship. It is the key to a bond that one shares deeply with, at best, very few others.[6]

'And now we can try to define friendship, as: enjoyment of the other's company, accord on many things, and mutual goodwill and liking. With the exception of wisdom I am inclined to think nothing better than this can be found in human experience.'[7] Some people would prefer to have riches, some to have health, some power, others honours, others again sensual pleasure – this last being what brutes most desire. And there are those who place the highest value on virtue – which is a noble view; but the examples of ideally perfect individuals given by, for example, the Stoics, are unrealistic models, and surpass the 'ordinary standard of life'.[8] But no life can be worth living without the mutual goodwill of a friend in it. There is 'nothing sweeter' than to have someone with whom one can talk as frankly and openly as if to oneself. The value of having someone to share both prosperity and adversity, enhancing the enjoyment of the former and lightening the burden of the latter, proves friendship's importance by itself.[9] Prosperity loses half its value if unshared, troubles are doubled without someone to comfort one. All those other desiderata – riches, health, status, pleasure – are single goods, but friendship encompasses everything: 'friendship embraces innumerable ends; turn where you will it is ever at your side; no barrier shuts it out; it is never untimely and never in the way.'[10]

The sovereign blessing of friendship is that it brightens hope for the future, and supports the friends themselves in their weakness and despair if these occur:

> In the face of a true friend we see a second self, so that where a man's friend is, he is; if his friend be rich, he is not poor; if he is weak, his friend's strength is his; and in his friend's life he enjoys a second life after his own is finished . . . If you should take the bond of friendship out of the world, no house or city could stand, nor would the soil even be tilled.[11]

A good way to see the value of friendship is to consider the contrasting case of families or states afflicted by animosities and divided by faction. They cannot avoid destruction. But all examples of loyalty in confronting danger are warmly applauded; only consider how rousingly the audience in the theatre greets the portrayal of true friendship. It is easy to see what a natural feeling friendship is given that it is so universally approved when displayed.[12]

Having anatomised friendship and pointed out how natural and deep-rooted its sources are, Laelius turns to consider the questions that press. Is the longing for friendship a function of weakness or want of means? Is it chiefly motivated by the desire to be able to get help when needed? Even if it is not quite that, is it nonetheless prompted by the utilitarian consideration that 'if you scratch my back, I'll scratch yours'? Or is there a more noble prior cause of friendship, which springs more directly from human nature?

At this point Laelius reminds his listeners that the word for friendship, *amicitia*, shares the same origin as the word for love, *amor*, 'for it is love that leads to the establishing of goodwill'.[13] It is true that advantages are sought and often obtained under the pretence of friendship, but in true friendship there is nothing false or pretended; it is genuine and spontaneous, springing not from need but from nature, 'from an inclination of the soul joined with a feeling of love'.[14]

This is not to deny that friendship is 'strengthened by the receipt of benefits and the desire to render service', but when these are prompted by prior amity and warmth of feeling they are very different from what is involved in base motivations towards gain.[15] If the latter were truly the origin of friendship, people would be inclined to friendship in proportion to the size of their wants and deficiencies. But the truth is the opposite: when a person is confident, fortified by virtue, and fully self-dependent, then is he 'most conspicuous for seeking out and maintaining friendship'.[16]

Perhaps conscious that the account being attributed to Laelius has begun to verge on the ideal, Cicero considers some realities. Not all friendships last: people change because of adversity or the burdens of age, their friendship might cease to be mutually beneficial, political differences might arise, rivalry in courtship or for office or for some other honour or advantage might drive them apart. One of the major causes of division occurs when one asks the other to do something wrong, 'as for example becoming an agent of vice or an abettor in violence'; in such cases friendship can turn to serious enmity.[17]

The question therefore arises, how far should one take loyalty to a friend? Cicero has Laelius rhetorically ask whether the friends of traitors to Rome should have stayed true to their friendship or to Rome, assuming an answer different from the one E. M. Forster said he hoped he would give: 'If I had to choose between betraying my country and betraying my friend, I hope I should have the guts to betray my country.' Forster goes on to cite Dante, who consigned Cassius and Brutus to the Inferno's lowest circle because they betrayed their friend Caesar rather than Rome.[18] But this is to underestimate the ferocity of patriotism as a Republican virtue in the eyes of Romans of Cicero's stamp; he has Laelius say that for 'crimes against the Republic' there will always be a 'heavy and righteous penalty'.[19]

From this Laelius concludes that it does not justify a sin that it was committed on behalf of a friend, and that therefore the following rule of friendship should be established: 'Neither ask dishonourable things, nor do them, if asked. And dishonourable it certainly is, and not to be allowed, for anyone to plead in defence of sins in general and especially of those against the State, that he committed them for the sake of a friend.'[20] Alternatively and positively phrased, this rule states:

Ask of friends only what is honourable; do for friends only what is honourable and without waiting to be asked; let zeal be ever present, but hesitation absent; dare to give true advice with all frankness; in friendship let the influence of friends who are wise counsellors be paramount, and let the influence be employed in advising, not only with frankness but, if the occasion demands, even with sternness.[21]

Up to this point Cicero has alluded to the views of others only in passing. But because there was an existing tradition of thought about the matter which would have been familiar to his readers (or hearers, given that these texts were often read to audiences), he next addresses some of the commoner ones directly. One view he deprecated was that people should not become too friendly with anyone, and not have too many friends, 'lest one man be full of anxiety for many'. Moreover, each has his own affairs to attend to, and it is an annoyance to be too involved in others' affairs; so it is 'best to hold the reins of friendship as loosely as possible, so that we may either draw them up or slacken them at will'. And all this advice is predicated on the idea that the best kind of life is one that is least full of care – and friendship brings cares.[22]

Laelius will have none of this. 'O noble philosophy! Why, they seem to take the sun out of the universe when they deprive life of friendship,' he says, and rejects the idea of 'freedom from care' as a failure to grasp that to flee from care is to flee from virtue, because kindness rejects ill will, bravery rejects cowardice, justice rejects injustice, and continence rejects excess. To care about being kind, brave and just is to accept the cares that come with contending against their opposites: accepting that care might come with what is worthwhile is appropriate. If we deprive the soul of the emotions associated with friendship we make ourselves no different from a stone.[23]

In rejecting the views of those who place *ataraxia* – peace of mind, an easy untroubled life – above friendship, or the possession of such goods as power or pleasure, Cicero has Laelius offer a contrast: who would wish to have unlimited wealth or pleasure on condition that he never felt for or received love from another person? 'Such indeed is the life of tyrants – a life, I mean, in which there can be no faith, no affection, no trust in the continuance of goodwill; where every act arouses suspicion and anxiety and where friendship has no place.'[24]

But if we are to accept that there are limits to friendship, boundaries beyond which one cannot go for a friend, what and where are they? Laelius begins by rejecting three suggestions on this head: that our feeling for our friends should be the same as our feeling for ourselves, that the degree of our goodwill towards them should match the degree of theirs to us; and that we should put the same value on our friends as we place on ourselves.[25] His reasons are that in the nature of friendship one friend will do for another things that he would not do for himself, that circumstances of life differ for different people so what is appropriate for one person is not for another, that to try placing an exact measure of equivalence on the mutualities of friendship involves a 'very close and petty accounting . . . I think true friendship is richer and more abundant than that and does not narrowly scan the reckoning lest it pay out more than it has received.'[26]

The last most exercises Laelius, who is emphatic that a friend should not value others and himself equally, as demonstrated by the case where one's friend is downcast or despairing: is one to have the same estimate of oneself, or should one not 'strive to rouse him up and lead him into a better train of thought and livelier hopes'?[27]

So where is the boundary? Well, *pace* what Laelius had to say earlier about the unacceptability of abetting a friend in committing treason or doing something dishonourable, he now says that loyalty requires that we should indeed help a friend even if it means 'turning aside from the straight path', just so long as doing so does not involve us in 'utter disgrace', and if it is a matter that involves the friend's life or reputation. Note that he says 'we *should* turn aside from the straight path'. But the possibility of disgrace offers at least an outer boundary, the 'limit to the indulgence which can be allowed to friendship': this is the one thing neither Laelius nor Cicero was prepared to contemplate even for a friend. Death, yes; disgrace, no.[28]

Evidently this is an aspect of the matter that gave Cicero difficulty. A few pages after this he talks about 'loyalty' and 'unswerving constancy' as the 'support and stay' of friendship,[29] which does not sit well either with the stricter or the laxer limits to friendship he has so far described. So he prefaces his talk of loyalty with a diversion into the need to choose one's friends carefully, testing them first: 'hence it is the part of wisdom to check the headlong rush of goodwill as we would that of a chariot, and thereby so manage friendship that we may in some

degree put the dispositions of friends, as we do those of ho
to a preliminary test'.[30] One such test is to see how a person
fares in matters of money transactions, or in ambition for
advancement in office; 'where can you find a man so high-
minded that he prefers his friend's advancement to his own?'[31]

This leads naturally to the question of what qualities a
potential friend should have, if he is to be one to whom
'unswerving constancy' can safely be pledged. The answer is
frankness, sociability, and sympathy, this last in the sense that
he is likely to resonate with the same interests and concerns as
oneself. The 'two rules of friendship' Laelius now lays down
can be adduced from this. First, there is to be 'no feigning or
hypocrisy', and second, be sure that the candidate for your
friendship is very constant, and reluctant to accept anything
said against you by others.[32]

A third rule is that there is to be equality in friendship,
whether the friendship be new or old – that is: a new friend is
to be treated equally with an old friend – and there is to be
equality between friends who are of unequal rank to each other
or to oneself, whether in office or the social hierarchy.

To guard against the ills that beset friendship – such as being
put into an awkward position over something dishonourable or
that might bring disgrace, or where the friendship is ending
because of political or other differences – it is, Laelius repeats,
best to enter friendships carefully: and in fact one should not
enter into friendships intended to be lasting and firm until one
has a degree of maturity. This, given the experience it brings,
allows one to give careful thought to the qualities of possible
friends, for one must aim to respect and revere as well as love
them, and they must therefore be worthy of both.[33]

Late in the dialogue Laelius has an apparent turn to the Aristotelian in saying, 'Everyone loves himself, not with a view of acquiring some profit for himself from his self-love, but because he is dear to himself on his own account; and unless the same feeling were transferred to friendship, the real friend would never be found; for he is, as it were, another self.'[34] It might be thought that the point being made here is cognate to the Christian one of 'loving one's neighbour as oneself' understood as implying that one must love oneself in order to be able to love one's neighbour well. And indeed there is something important in this thought. According to phrasing, this adjuration does not necessarily amount to saying that one's friend is literally another self, in the sense of being exactly like oneself, but rather (and much more plausibly) that one's friend is to be treated with the same concern and interest as one treats oneself. There is as usual something reflex about invocation of the 'another self' trope, yet the whole tenor of Cicero's account is premised on what is surely an appropriate recognition of the difference and otherness of a friend, whom one nevertheless values, respects, and even indeed needs, for the mixture of reasons Cicero has astutely assembled: the natural impetus we feel towards friendship based on shared interests and congeniality, and the fact that friends do not invariably have a parity of feelings towards each other, or equal goodwill, or hold one another to be of exactly commensurate value. In fact these were three requirements imposed by other philosophical views that Cicero rejects, as noted above; and in the rejection of them lies the implied recognition that friends are separate and different, and that their friendship is a function of how those differences mesh and provide mutual satisfactions, not for instrumental reasons but out of the goodwill that the parties bear each other.

There is a fallacy in informal logic known as the 'no true Scotsman' fallacy, derived from the claim some Scottish patriot might make on hearing of a fellow Scot's turpitude: 'no true Scotsman would do such a thing.' The fallacy resides in so defining a 'true X' that if some putative X fails to fit the desired definition, it can be excluded from the class of Xs by moving the goal posts so that they only compass 'true' Xs. This fallacy is committed by Laelius early on when he says 'true friendship can only exist between good people', which allows him to say of evil people who are fast friends that theirs is not 'true' friendship. The point is an important one for those who make it, because the classical trope that 'true' friendship requires mutually recognised virtue allows theoreticians of friendship to escape certain problems, for example the one about loyalty being an essential feature of friendship, which conflicts with the requirement that friendship should not lead people into dishonourable acts. The problem can be avoided by the stipulation that 'true' friendship is predicated on virtue, and that therefore it would never lead the parties into dishonour – not only because a 'true' friend would not ask you to commit a dishonourable deed, nor because a 'true' friend would abet you in dishonourable activities but, rather, would remonstrate with you and lead you into better ways; but because you would not become friends with a dishonourable person in the first place, given that 'true' friendship is not possible with one such. Since this is obviously not the case, talk of 'true' friendship is destined to mislead.

Laelius' definition of a 'good person' as one who is honourable, just, generous, courageous, loyal, and free from greed, intemperance and violence, is prefaced by his saying that he is not going to become enmeshed in 'pedantic accuracy' in defining what we mean by 'a good person'. But the standard he sets here is extremely high, and is conventional rather than – as Cicero claims he wishes to be – pragmatic. One thing that we would hope a friend to be (a 'true' friend!) is somewhat forgiving and tolerant of our faults, our failings and failures, our imperfections, and even at times our downright sins. Of course it is too much to expect that a friendship might survive genuine nastiness directed by one party at another or others, unless there are extenuating circumstances; but as with the path of 'true' love, it is utopian to expect that a friendship will always be trouble-free.

Laelius' definition of 'friendship' itself – enjoyment of the other's company, accord on many things, and mutual goodwill and liking – fares much better than his definitions of 'true friendship' and 'good person', and has exactly the sensible ring that one expects from Cicero. The notion of *benevolentia*, 'goodwill', includes within it that of a commitment to sharing adversity as well as prosperity, to supporting one's friend in 'weakness and despair' as well as in the pleasures of life; if the phrase 'true friendship' has work to do, it does it here.

Like Aristotle, but even more explicitly – and no doubt because of the influence of the Stoic philosophers with their famous exhortation to 'follow nature' which, although he was not a Stoic, he was evidently impressed by – Cicero sees the impulse to friendship as natural, a necessitating feature of human nature just as it is of animal nature in general. But the social factors are as powerful if not more so: once the feeling of goodwill and the sentiment of affection are engaged, they can be strengthened by mutual benefits, or weakened by the occurrence of divisions or change of character or personality over time. All this makes sense. It is a recognition that the classical conception's impossible ideal of friendship between impossibly ideal individuals needs tempering by a healthy dose of pragmatism to make it anywhere near plausible.

It is not possible to leave antiquity – still less, its lessons for our own time – without mention of Plutarch and the question he raises about having too many friends.[35] This is a point of relevance to us today because of the huge numbers of 'friends' that people acquire on such social media as Facebook. If one has ten, fifty, a hundred, a thousand 'friends' on Facebook, are they all friends? If they are, are they all equally friends? Does the distinction between friends and acquaintances take on a particular significance in the Facebook age? As with at least some other matters of significance, the ancient world is not without insights.

Plutarch is better known for his *Parallel Lives* than his *Moral Essays*, but some of these latter have great charm and interest – not least on this matter of how many friends can really be friends.

In Plutarch's view, one major obstacle to acquiring a really good friend is the desire for many friends, which is the product of our love of novelty and our fickleness and inconstancy, so that we are forever pursuing new friendships even though they come to nothing.[36] He points out that literature teaches us that exemplary friendships all consist in the relationship between a pair, and cites the examples of Theseus and Pirithous, Achilles and Patroclus, Orestes and Pylades, Phintias and Damon,

Epaminondas and Pelopidas. And he observes that the Aristotelian 'another self' idea itself implies duality.[37]

The only coin that can purchase a good friend, Plutarch says, is 'benevolence and complaisance conjoined with virtue'. But these are rare qualities, so if one has a superfluity of friends they are unlikely to be well endowed with them. Just as a river divided into many courses runs with a feeble stream in each, so if one's affection is divided among too many recipients it will be weak and ineffective.[38]

Plutarch says he is not insisting that we should each have just one friend, but that we should aim to have one pre-eminent friend. A friend should be chosen with judgement, so that one can 'rejoice in his company, and make use of him in need', which is not possible if one has too many so-called friends. For a friend should be virtuous, pleasant company, and useful, and to judge whether he will be all three we need to be as thoughtful in our choice as we are when picking a tutor for our children or a new member of a choir, whom we need to hear sing so that we can be sure he will harmonise with the others. It is far more difficult than either of these two last tasks 'to meet with many friends who will take off their coats to aid you in every fortune, each of whom "offers his services to you in prosperity, and does not object to share your adversity"'.[39]

Like Polonius in his advice to Hamlet – 'Do not dull thy palm with entertainment of each new-hatch'd, unfledg'd comrade' – Plutarch advises strongly against too-ready intimacy with chance comers or flatterers; 'what is easily got is not always desirable'; the beginning of a friendship is key to the quality of its continuance.[40] A bad friend is not easily got rid of, troublesome if kept, harmful if turned into an enemy in the process of being shaken off; 'as in the case of food which is injurious or harmful, we cannot retain it on the stomach without damage and hurt, nor can we expel it as it was taken into the mouth, but only in a putrid, mixed and changed form ... if he be got rid of forcibly it is with hostility and hatred, and like the voiding of bile.'[41]

In short: one must choose one's friends very carefully, and must take one's time in doing it. 'As therefore Zeuxis, when some people accused him of painting slowly, said, I admit that I do, but then I paint to last.'[42]

Plutarch seems unabashedly to run contrary to Aristotle and Cicero in thinking that a good friend is one who affords pleasure and usefulness. But like them he means that the bond between friends, 'strengthened by intercourse and kindness', is what produces both; it is these that prompt what friendship brings, not the other way round. 'As Menelaus said about Odysseus, "Nor did anything ever divide or separate us, who loved and delighted in one another, till death's black cloud over-shadowed us".'[43] Such depth of feeling between friends is not the outcome of calculation.

Steadiness and constancy are the desiderata of friendship, given that once the bond is established the parties will share in each other's difficulties as well as in their good times. That is yet another reason for choosing with care, given the rarity of those qualities. 'The soul suitable for many friendships must be impressionable, and versatile, pliant, and changeable. But friendship requires a steady, constant and unchangeable character, a person that is uniform in his intimacy. And so a constant friend is a thing rare and hard to find.'[44] It can be turned round too, pointing out that as we do well to choose one or a very few friends with care, so our own capacity for friendship towards them demands it likewise – for consider the implication of the old English proverb, 'A friend to all is a friend to none.'

This is sensible plain advice, obvious enough, but entertainingly put. If anything it is slightly less precious than the idealised conceptions of the major classic sources; and that is a step in the right direction.

CHAPTER 4

Christianity and Friendship

One of the most influential works Cicero wrote in his years of maximum philosophical productivity was a dialogue called *Hortensius*, named for his friend Quintus Hortensius Hortalus. It was an introductory survey of philosophy, intended to lay before the Roman Republic the wealth of the Greek philosophical tradition. It is taken to be an adaptation and expansion of Aristotle's own introduction to philosophy, known in Latin as the *Protrepticus philosophiae*, a work famous in antiquity as an invitation to philosophical life and thought.

Both works, alas, are lost; only fragments of them remain. Some efforts have been made to reconstruct the *Protrepticus* from quotations of it in ancient texts. But it is Cicero's *Hortensius* which had the greater known impact, and in no less a case than that of Augustine of Hippo.

Augustine tells us in his *Confessions* that it was reading Cicero's *Hortensius* at the age of nineteen that filled him with a 'burning ardour' for philosophy.[1] It was another decade before his life of wine and women gave way to a Christian conversion, but he always counted Cicero as one of his chief influences – along with Plato, Plotinus and Porphyry: a formidable group – a claim confirmed by his saying in old age that 'there is no greater consolation than the loyalty and mutual love' of friends.[2]

The fourth book of Augustine's *Confessions* contains his account of friendship. One of its interesting features is that there is, at the outset, an obvious difficulty for Christians in thinking about friendship, given that their religion's founder enjoins them to *agape*, indiscriminate love for their fellow human beings. Christianity is not alone in this prescription; Buddhism and Mohism likewise exhort universal love for one's fellows (and in the case of Buddhism, even more widely and compassionately, for all things). But any such view is incompatible with a selective and preferential love for one or a few others, elevated above the rest of humankind by the special place they hold in one's affections. These thoughts by themselves would seem immediately to imply that one should not have friends as such, in order to be a friend to all; and then one falls foul of the criticisms Plutarch levelled at those who have too many friends.

In the case of Augustine the dilemma was the more acute because of the friendship he enjoyed with a youth who had been his schoolfellow and playmate and was now living with him in his home town of Tagaste, to which he had returned as a teacher of rhetoric. 'Like myself, he was just rising up in the flower of youth . . . it was a sweet friendship, being ripened by the zeal of common studies.'[3] Writing in Christian retrospect, Augustine had to qualify this by saying it was not a 'true friendship' (the 'no true Scotsman' again) because only friend-ships bound by God through the Holy Spirit can be such; but he adds, 'my soul could not exist without him', their friendship being 'sweeter to me than all the sweetness of my life thus far'.[4] The young man died of a fever:

> My heart was utterly darkened by this sorrow and every-where I looked I saw death . . . All the things I had done with him, now that he was gone, became a frightful torment. My eyes sought him everywhere, but they did not see him; and I hated all places because he was not in them, because they could not say to me, 'Look, he is coming' . . . [when I asked my soul] 'hope thou in God' she did not obey, because that dearest friend I had lost was an actual man, both truer and better than the imagined deity I ordered her to put her hope in. Nothing but tears comforted me and they took my friend's place in my heart's yearning.[5]

The agony Augustine suffered over his lost friend drove him from Tagaste to Carthage so that he could escape the scene of his grief. In time the grief abated, and 'what revived and refreshed me, more than anything else, was the consolation of other friends, with whom I went on loving the things I loved', though not (as Augustine retrospectively laments) God himself. Then he gives the following superb account:

> to discourse and jest with him; to indulge in courteous exchanges; to read pleasant books together; to trifle together; to be earnest together; to differ at times without ill-humour,

as a man might do with himself, and even through these infrequent dissensions to find zest in our more frequent agreements; sometimes teaching, sometimes being taught; longing for someone absent with impatience and welcoming the homecomer with joy. These and similar tokens of friendship, which spring spontaneously from the hearts of those who love and are loved in return – in countenance, tongue, eyes, and a thousand ingratiating gestures – were all so much fuel to melt our souls together, and out of the many made us one.[6]

Superb.

This is, though, a noticeably secular account. 'This is what we love in our friends,' Augustine says; 'and we love it so much that a man's conscience accuses itself if he does not love one who loves him, or responds in love to love, seeking nothing from the other but the evidences of his love. This is the source of our moaning when one's friend dies – the gloom of sorrow, the steeping of the heart in tears, all sweetness turned to bitterness – and the feeling of death in the living, because of the loss of the life of the dying.'[7] Immediately after these words Augustine writes a long prayer, as if making it up to the deity for the fact that he loved his friends better than he loved him. A dithyramb to God obliges him to end by saying, 'These things I did not understand at that time [the time of those friendships], and I loved those inferior beauties.'[8]

But the key dilemma for the Christian is tucked away in the very first line of the prayer: 'Blessed is he who loves thee, and who loves his friend in thee, and his enemy also, for thy sake;

for he alone loses none dear to him, if all are dear to Him who cannot be lost.'[9] If our greatest love is to be reserved to God, then to love another human too much, or more than God, is wrong. It is moot how much love for anyone other than God is left over if we are to love God 'with all our heart and all our might', as the adjuration has it; but anyway such love has to be experienced 'through God'. But we are to love our enemies as well as our friends; we are to love everyone; 'love thy neighbour as thyself' is the second of the new commandments issued by Christ, and in answer to the question 'Who is my neighbour?' the answer is given in the Good Samaritan story about complete strangers.[10] In the passionate and moving letters of Héloïse to Abélard after their misfortunes, the power of human love is as well displayed as in Augustine's pre-conversion friendships; both Abélard's po-faced responses and Augustine's post-conversion regrets illustrate the reverse.[11]

Yet the story of friendship in Augustine did not end with his conversion. In fact the *Confessions* makes it clear that as well as Ambrose of Milan it was his friends Nebridius and Alypius who were his companions on the road to conversion and thereafter. Of Alypius, alongside whom he was baptised and who became bishop of Tagaste when he was himself bishop of Hippo, Augustine wrote, 'he was the brother of my heart . . . anyone who knows us would say that he and I are distinct individuals in body only, not in mind; I mean in our harmoniousness and trusty friendship.'[12] This is the attestation of someone for whom friendship is a matter of great human significance, which all the obeisance to a third party (viz. the deity) in the relationship does not change; one could edit out the apostrophes to the deity and be left with a marvellous rendering of what friendship means to someone with an evident genius for it.

At times, indeed, Augustine himself seems impatient with the implication of the divine demand that we give our total concentration to the task of obedience, for there is this world and our unignorable existence in it to be dealt with: 'Two things are essential in this world – life, and friendship. Both must be prized highly, and not undervalued. They are nature's gifts. We were created by God that we might live; but if we are not to live solitarily, we must have friendship.'[13] And again,

> The love in friendship should be given freely. The reason you have a friend and love him ought not to be that he can do something for you; if you love him so that you can get money or some other advantage from him, then you are not really loving him, you are loving what you can get by his means. A friend is to be loved freely, for his own sake, not for the sake of something else.[14]

One might note that the 'something else' could equally be the approval of a deity, and one might note also that to love a friend because doing so is required by God is not to love freely. Again, it would seem to be wisdom, not God, that places value on friendship, if a remark in a letter to Proba is taken at face value: 'So to these two things that are so necessary in this world, well-being and friendship, along came Wisdom as a visitor.'[15]

But of course Augustine's official position is, as it has to be, that 'true' friendship is 'of God'; 'You only love your friend truly, after all, when you love God in your friend, either because he is in him, or in order that he may be in him . . . there is no true friendship unless God welds it between souls that cling together by the love poured into their hearts by the Holy Spirit.'[16] This was the major theme of the converted Augustine, and the tension between love of God and love of human friends was resolved in the piety that it is God who forges the friendships in the first place. And it had better be so, Augustine admonishes, for if friendship is allowed to be wholly secular, it can lead us astray: 'The bond of human friendship has a sweetness of its own, binding many souls into one. Yet because of these values, sin is committed, because we have an inordinate preference for these goods of a lower order and neglect the better and the higher good.'[17] What he had in mind was the 'unfriendly friendship' that had led him to steal pears as a boy: blaming his companions for leading him astray, he famously recounts the occasion on which he stole pears from a neighbour's farm, pears that were not very tempting to look at or eat, so that it was not the fruit itself but the mere pleasure of the adventure that counted, because it was forbidden. 'Looking back I am now certain that I would not have done it had I been alone. Maybe what I really loved was the companionship of the friends with whom I did it . . . Oh unfriendly friendship!'[18]

The finished doctrine of friendship in Augustine is unimpeachably a theological one. 'There can be no full and true agreement about human things among friends who disagree about divine things, for it necessarily follows that one who despises divine things esteems human things more than he ought, and that whoever does not love God who made man, has not learned to love man rightly.'[19] The two commandments of Christ are given this gloss:

> You shall love the Lord your God with your whole heart and soul and with all your mind; you shall love your neighbour as yourself; so, regarding the first, there is agreement on divine matters, regarding the second, there is goodwill and love; if you and your friend hold fast to these two commandments, your friendship will be true and eternal, uniting you not only to each other but to the Lord himself.[20]

The question whether human friendships are only 'true' friendships if forged by God and enjoyed by mutually encouraging Christians is a 'true Scotsman' question, of course, because it is an act of legislation to say that heretics or atheists, or followers of a different religion altogether, who love each other and are fast and loyal friends, are 'not really' friends, or indeed 'unfriendly friends' (and thus enemies) because they encourage each other in the continuance of their mistakes. We soon get led into paradox when we note that if those who are outside the pale of Christian fellowship love their 'unfriendly friends', then they are obeying the injunction to love their enemies; and that is no mere sophism.

But the complication is greater in connection with enemies, for Augustine eventually has to find means to deal with the problem that we are ordered by God to love our enemies as well as our friends, thus blurring the boundary between what we owe to friends and what significantly cannot be owed to enemies, as it were by definition: these are friends, those are enemies; there is a fundamental difference. But they must both be loved; therefore he needs to draw a distinction between the two kinds of loving, and does it this way: 'Moreover, how can that [i.e. love] be denied to friends which is due even to enemies? To enemies, however, this debt is paid with caution, whereas to friends it is repaid with confidence.'[21]

Such are the difficulties which the necessity of conforming to dogma imposes. If we detach the account in *Confessions* Book IV from the theological overlay, we get a remarkably warm human portrait of the relationship that Augustine, with Cicero, recognised as central to life as actually lived in the real world: 'to discourse and jest with [one's friend]; to indulge in courteous exchanges; to read pleasant books together; to trifle together; to be earnest together; to differ at times without ill-humour; to find zest in our agreements; sometimes teaching, sometimes being taught; longing for him when absent and welcoming him home with joy . . . This is what we love in our friends . . . seeking nothing from the other but the evidences of his love.'[22] By any standard that has to be part of what we mean when we speak of friendship.

What Augustine does not address, and what Aquinas does, is the question of friendship – if that remains the right word – between profoundly unequal beings: humans and God. It might seem surprising that friendship should be regarded by anyone as quite the right relationship to be considering in relation to the putative creator, master and commander of the universe, to whom the appropriate attitude is so often said to be worship, submission and obedience, hardly the stuff of chumminess. But this indeed is what St Thomas Aquinas says.

We do well first to consider the difficulties. In Aristotle a condition of friendship is equality and shared activity and interests; neither equality nor sharing is possible in the human–God relationship. In all of Aristotle, Cicero and Augustine the reliance that friends place on each other is a feature of the reciprocity distinctive of friendship; but what reciprocity is there with the deity? Can even the holiest and most faithful epigone of God rely, for example, on his answering a call for some sort of present help? The inferior party to this relationship is largely ignorant of God's nature, and wholly ignorant of God's view of things and purposes; how can Aquinas even contemplate describing the human–divine relationship in terms of friendship?

And yet, in the scattered places where the subject comes up in Aquinas, he sets himself that task: he takes it that human friendships provide analogies for, and further provide models of and staging-posts towards, the human–divine relationship – which anyway in its perfected and final state is, according to Aquinas, intended to be a friendship in a quite straightforward sense of the term.

In the *Summa theologiae* Aquinas places friendship among the goods that go to constitute a happy life.[23] The happy person does not need friends either for assistance or for pleasure, because as he is otherwise virtuous (he would not be happy unless he were so) he is self-sufficient and has all the enjoyment he needs from being conscious of his virtue. But friends are indeed necessary; he needs them so that he can engage in virtuous activities, including being able to exercise benevolence towards them.[24]

Aquinas' basic anatomy of the different kinds of love we can bear others follows Aristotle's in distinguishing genuine friendship, in which the parties love one another for themselves and desire the other's good, from relationships predicated on utility or pleasure.[25] The former is friendship love, the latter is concupiscent love; the two kinds of love, often overlapping in practice, are the causes of all human action and feeling.[26]

The appearance of conflict between charity and friendship – that is, between universal brotherly love, *agape*, and the partial, preferential affection of friendship – which bedevils Christian thinking about the latter does not appear to be a problem for Aquinas. Somewhat like Augustine he takes the route of differentiating between orders of intensity of charity, the hierarchy allowing a preferential form of charity to be focused on just one or a few others, which can survive even in our 'homeland,' *patria*, meaning heaven.[27]

The problem of charity is framed by the assertion in Luke 6: 32 that 'If you love those who love you, what credit is that to you? For even sinners love those who love them.' In order to substantiate the claim that Christian charity is human friendship elevated by grace to a new status, Aquinas quotes John 15: 15, 'I do not call you servants any longer . . . I call you friends.' On this view, charity is the perfected and spiritual version of what in their inadequate corporeal way human beings achieve in friendship.[28]

It is not clear that the words from John's Gospel quite do what Aquinas intends. More fully quoted from verses 14–15 they say, 'You are my friends if you do what I command. I do not call you servants any longer, because a servant does not know what his master is doing.' This rather better fits the special sense of 'friendship' that would apply if this were a factual state of affairs; but it is not friendship in any other recognisable sense.

A yet larger problem looms for Aquinas, however: how can charity towards an enemy be accounted a type of friendship, given Aristotle's requirement that friendship involves reciprocated love? Aquinas's solution is a paradigm of the kind of reasoning required to reconcile Athens and Jerusalem: we love our enemies *indirectly*, says Aquinas, through a chain of people whose love for friends eventually arrives at one's enemy. Thus, I love you, you love your friend whom I do not love or even perhaps know, that person loves someone else . . . and so on until the enemy is reached by an intermediary chain of lovings.[29]

And our enemies love us back by this same indirect route. In any case, all charity in fact has God as its 'formal object and not merely its end', which obviates the further difficulty that to love a sinner or an enemy (however indirectly or – a different problem yet again – inadvertently) might in some sense be to condone what makes them so.[30] In the case of sinners, this cannot be right; for Aristotle required that we should love only those who are virtuous, and that honour is a prerequisite for anyone to be lovable as a friend. How can one love the sinner, even granting that we do not love the sin? Once again, this problem is solved by making God the 'formal object' of our love. Thus in loving the sinner we are loving God, and therefore we love something virtuous and honourable after all.

But it does not solve the problem of God's love for us, because we are emphatically not virtuous or honourable. How can he love us, if our being virtuous is a requirement for our being lovable? In this case we are told that God's loving us is a function of his virtue, not ours: his loving us makes us good, he does not love us because we are good.[31]

In this barrage of casuistries there is an interesting remark that lends additional subtlety to the Aristotelian observation that appropriate self-love is required for one to be a good friend to another. Aquinas quotes Leviticus 19:18 'love your friend as yourself', and uses it to introduce a twist to the 'another self' trope: if we cannot be good friends to ourselves, how can we be good friends to others? If we have no self-respect, how can we expect our friends to respect us, and in that case to be our friends at all? The point is a good one, though it can be taken to extremes: there is a now-standard trope in our own times, the 'because I'm worth it' trope, that shows how self-love can become a justification for not even seeing the existence of others, especially the less fortunate. Self-respect is one thing, egoism another; the ancient authors are thinking of the former rather than the latter.

The principal difficulty for a commentator on religious views about so human and sublunary, yet so necessary and important, a matter as friendship is that whereas some good things might be said in the course of them – as is manifestly the case with Augustine, a man of strong human passions and experience of their exercise – their subordination to doctrine much devalues them. The problem was stated by Russell in connection with Aquinas: that when conclusions are antecedently given, or when at the very least one knows that they have to be consistent with conclusions antecedently given, the value of arguments leading to them is minimal.[32]

As is usual with doctrine, though, epigones live a double mental life: the doctrine says one thing, human interests and needs assert themselves nevertheless – as with Roman Catholics and contraception. The importance of friendship to human beings leads to people making friends independently of theory or doctrine, and even to creating theory and doctrine which are at odds with official theory and doctrine.

Look at any Christian website on friendship and we see familiar things being said: friends help each other in times of need, share the joys and sorrows of life, trust each other, forgive each other, share aspirations and goals and encourage each other to realise them.[33] The idea that one's love for others should be universal and should not single out any one person more than another would not merely be unacceptable but unlivable, exactly like the Gospel teaching which says that if we really wish to follow Christ we must give away all our money and possessions and, like the lilies of the field, make no plans for the morrow. The most consistent and honest of epigones is regarded as a zealot for doing what the scriptures of the major religions actually say; if everyone were zealot enough, human life would be intolerable, but (mercifully, perhaps) would not last long anyway.

Even for a devout believer it is hard to see what difference would be made to her friendships if the moral theology attending the concept of them were stripped away. What does it add to Augustine's striking account of the nature of a warm and loving friendship to say that the parties to it were brought together by a deity, as in an arranged marriage? The fact is that the endeavours of Augustine and Aquinas were necessitated by the problem that this wholly secular phenomenon was too likely to be disruptive of the idea that there is nothing good but what is from God, and therefore has to be accommodated by means of some intricate argumentation. Like the deities of the countrymen (the 'pagans') it had to be habilitated into the ambit of the faith, just as the popular winter solstice celebrations of antiquity had to be transformed into Christmas. And thus we see what Augustine and Aquinas respectively make of the task; were we to compare their efforts we might say that Augustine wins by a country mile.

CHAPTER 5

Renaissance Friendship

In the face of entrenched historical labels we are bound to enter the usual disclaimers: that the three or more centuries lumped together as 'The Renaissance' were internally as diverse as any unlabelled three centuries could be, and that we obscure as much as illuminate by giving it a capitalised name. At the same time we are bound to notice contrasts with the preceding high medieval period, 'medieval' being the name chosen by Petrarch, one of the fathers of the Renaissance, to denote what he saw as the gulf separating his time from a world in which life in the flesh was regarded as a vale of tears, a dark and dangerous antechamber to the felicity promised those who could endure it with as little stain of sin on their souls as possible. Such medieval literature as there was on the subject of how to live was in the *contemptus mundi* genre, warning that the devil and his minions were lurking in wait to take every opportunity – even the opportunity of a sneeze! – to snatch your soul down to everlasting perdition.

This ugly view – whose upside was the soaring beauty of Gothic cathedrals pointing to the sky as if to lift away from earth's filth and fly upwards – was replaced by the Renaissance's celebration of life in the here and now. Medieval art is relentlessly religious; its happiest manifestation is the endlessly iterated iconography of that successor to a goddess of lost or more likely suppressed memory, the Madonna[1] – or the prelude to her, the Annunciation. But its majority manifestation is flagellation, crucifixion, deposition, entombment, the suffering on and at the foot of the cross, depictions of hell and its torments designed to frighten the onlooker,[2] with the occasional more positive note of resurrection and ascension thrown in.

By contrast, Renaissance art gives us landscapes and picnics in them, portraits of ordinary (of course, rich or powerful; but not divine) people, still lives, mythological subjects, erotic subjects, nudes, battle scenes, animals, a wider variety of narratives from biblical and literary sources illuminating aspects of human life and destiny, and much besides. With the art came poetry and music, a revolution in architecture to provide ampler housing for life in the empirical present, the beginnings of renewed enquiry in science and philosophy, increased literacy, and travel; indeed, in the voyages of Portuguese explorers at this time lay the beginning of globalisation. All these things were inspired directly or otherwise by the recovery of the classical past, by the rebirth of attitudes and practices which centuries of religious dominance had rather successfully managed to obscure and in many cases to obliterate.

Petrarch's contemporary and friend Giovanni Boccaccio, standing on the threshold of the Renaissance, wrote this at the end of his Tenth Day story of Titus and Gisippus in the *Decameron*:

> Friendship, then, is a most sacred thing, worthy not only of singular reverence but of being commended with perpetual praise, as the most discreet mother of liberality and honour, the sister of gratitude and charity, the enemy of hatred and avarice, ever ready, without waiting to be asked, to do virtuously to another what it would wish done to itself. Its sacred results are today most rarely to be seen in two persons, by the fault and to the shame of men's miserable cupidity which makes them look only to their own interests; so friendship has been driven to the ends of the earth and left in perpetual exile.[3]

Neither the story itself nor this peroration invokes religious grounds or sanctions. It was written a century after Aquinas's discussion of friendship, but bears no marks of that or any other theology. It is, in both the then contemporary and today's contemporary senses, humanist in character.

This was a promising start, and the Renaissance is full of examples of celebration of secular friendship as a chief value of the age. Perhaps inevitably, however, the great majority of those references are mere iterations of each other, and, worse, almost all involve repeating the one remark in Aristotle which, arguably, should least define what friends are to each other: the 'another self' remark.[4] Its ubiquity of quotation makes it a cliché of the Renaissance. This fact has not done much to add to the quality or interest of the great flowering of 'Renaissance friendship studies' noted by Christopher Marlow in his survey of the subject, and which he explains by the latitude it offers for cross-disciplinary research.[5] A cynic might say that academics in search of something to do in these fields have developed a tortured and prolix way of writing presumably intended to give an impression of scholarship, depth and originality, which does not help matters: but in this case the matters are not much to be helped anyway, for Plato's *Lysis*, Aristotle's *Nicomachean Ethics* and Cicero's *De amicitia* were the set texts, and 'another self' was the key quotation; to know this is to know all. Meanwhile in practice the idea of a 'friend' in the functional sense of a coadjutor, colleague, supporter, kinsman and anyone who is 'with us because not against us' continued to demonstrate that the literary and philosophical sense of 'friend' was still an idealisation as it had been in those classical texts, and entered into the discourse of literates as an affectation, for example in the high-flown language of the consciously literary letter, where the feelings of both writer and addressee are couched in passionate terms.

A pivotal moment in the dissemination of the *amicus alter ipse* trope must be John Tiptoft's 1481 translation of Cicero's *De amicitia* for the Caxton Press.[6] The sayings of Erasmus – the *Collectanea* of 1500 and *Adagiorum chiliades* of 1508 – were hugely popular in the sixteenth century, and scores of them relate to friendship, iterating the classical sources in a variety of disguises: 'a friend is another self' and 'friendship is equality', 'between friends all is owned in common', and so on. But these were not always merely rhetorical flourishes; Erasmus enjoyed famous friendships with Sir Thomas More and Hans Holbein, and even wrote a dialogue under the title *Amicitia*, although as this has more to do with the natural sympathies and antipathies of animals (how the lizard hates the snake, for example), it devotes hardly any space to human friendship. A lesson Erasmus draws, however, is that liking and aversion are inexplicably the work of something natural in us, and so we must seek our friends among those 'towards whom we feel a propensity', there being no trumping reason.[7]

The 'another self' trope appears in every notable source. Thomas Elyot's *The Boke Named The Governour* (1531) has 'a frende is properly named of Philosphers the other I'; Richard Taverner's *The Garden of Wysdom* (1539) reports that when Aristotle was asked 'what a frende is, One soule (quoth) he, in two bodyes'; a poem attributed to Nicholas Grimald in *Tottel's Miscellany* (1557–87) has the couplet 'Behold thy friend, and of thyself thy pattern see;/One soul, a wonder shall it seem, in bodies twain to be.'[8]

And so it goes on. The 1580s saw a veritable rush of publications on friendship, for example Walter Dorke's *A Tipe or Figure of Friendship, wherein is livelie, and compendiouslie expressed, the right nature and propertie of a perfect and true friend* (1589), Thomas Churchyard's *A Sparke of Friendship and warme goodwill, that shewest the effect of true affection and unfoldes the finenesse of this world* (1588), and Thomas Breme's *The mirror of friendship: both how to know a perfect friend, and how to choose him* (1584).[9] Given that none of these texts offers startlingly new insights into their subject, it is evident that there was a good deal of recycling going on – of one another, Erasmus, and the ancients. The endlessly repeated points are 'another self'; 'equality'; 'all things in common';

'agreement'; and all concur that the 'sweete communication' of friendship is a 'consolation' and a 'most cordiall medicine'.[10]

It is easy and instructive to turn to Shakespeare and the dramatists to find windows to peer through into current conceptions of friendship in the period. Consider briefly just one – but a pertinent – example: *Timon of Athens*. It is a portrait not so much of false friendship as of the effect of disappointment writ large. What Timon gave and did not receive in return is not the point, nor even that he did not receive in return, for case-by-case reciprocity does not have to be automatic. Rather, the point is that in his need he was refused, when he had refused nothing even to those not in need. The injustice, betrayal and devastating failure of friendship's assumed bond of reciprocal commitment are what underlie Timon's rage against humankind. The character of Timon, questionable though it is first in its profligate folly and then in its generalisation of hatred against all when it was only some who betrayed him, nevertheless provides an interesting hook for a remark by William Hazlitt: that in this play Shakespeare seems unwaveringly in earnest throughout. Because the crux is what false friends do to Timon, there has to be a premise that friendship is about the opposite of falsities: that it is or should be about mutuality, help, trust and the keeping of an implicit contract, at least. None of these things holds in *Timon*, which is why Timon falls.

The two discursive texts on friendship that have survived from the period as part of an educated person's reading today, are both late Renaissance contributions whose authors are famous for other reasons. They are essays by Montaigne and Bacon respectively entitled 'On Friendship' and 'Of Friendship'.

Each of them is substantial in content, but they are very different. Montaigne regarded his feelings for his dead friend Etienne de La Boétie as special, out of the ordinary, not like common friendship and indeed of a kind that very few would be capable of experiencing – even though he was not immune to the general contagion: he says friendship is 'one soul in two bodies, according to the fit definition of Aristotle'. But so great was his feeling for his lost friend that he did not claim resemblance for it to what constituted the great friendships of myth and antiquity; he seems to have felt that it surpassed even them.

Bacon's essay, by contrast, while full of meat and good observation, is addressed to the question of what friendship does – its 'fruits', as he calls them. The difference between the two essays arises from the difference of temperament and purpose between their two authors. Montaigne wrote out of his private feelings, Bacon saw himself as an educator of mankind: theirs is the difference between the subjective and the objective impulse to communicate ideas.[11]

It is interesting to note that Montaigne's 'Of Friendship' appeared in the second book of his essays, published together with the first book in 1580, and his essay 'On Three Kinds of Relationships' appeared in the third book, published in 1588; and that in speaking of friendship in the latter he is not quite as exclusive as he had made himself out to be in the former. Indeed, he even regrets that he is not so formed as to be capable of enjoying easy acquaintanceships with all sorts and conditions of people, including the carpenters and gardeners on his estate; he envies those able to strike up a casual conversation with them.[12]

Having acknowledged that his retiring demeanour in company might have lost him the goodwill of many, Montaigne proceeds to claim that nevertheless he has 'a great aptitude for acquiring and retaining rare and admirable friendships. Since I grasp very eagerly at any acquaintance that is to my liking, I make such advances, and rush so eagerly forward, that I rarely fail to attach myself and to make an impression where I strike. I have often had happy proof of this.'[13] Alluding to the great friendship when younger with Etienne de La Boétie, he says that he has learned that friendship is 'for companionship not for the herd' (here quoting Plutarch), and that he cannot abide those imperfect and commonplace friendships which result from the parties to them not giving themselves to each other wholeheartedly.[14]

In criticising himself for not being apt for easy acquaint-anceships Montaigne also criticises Plato for saying that a master should always speak as a master and never as a familiar to his servants. Montaigne's honourable reason is that 'it is inhuman and unjust to lay so much stress on this chance prerogative of fortune'.[15] But this is not friendship, although it is not *noblesse oblige* either; it is that great but simple good thing, humanity. This in turn suggests that there is a distinction in the offing between the desire to be well disposed to all others – our humanity towards them – and the particular needs we have for friends. In this later essay Montaigne describes those needs in less exigent terms than Aristotle, or Aristotle's more zealous followers, would countenance.

The account Montaigne proceeds to give is a down-to-earth one, despite beginning with what seems a demanding require-ment. 'The men whose society and intimacy I seek are those who are called well-bred and talented men; and the thought of these gives me a distaste for others. Their kind is, rightly considered, the rarest that we have, a kind that owes almost everything to nature.'[16] To nature, he says, and therefore not education; but we had better register here that 'good breeding' is not a gift of nature. There are kindly and noble people whom we might call 'nature's gentlefolk', but that is a different matter; Montaigne might have found them among his gardeners, and in this account they are not in his library with him sitting beside his fire.

'The purpose of our intercourse,' he continues, 'is simply intimacy, familiarity, and talk; the exercise of the mind is our sole gain. In our conversations all subjects are alike to me. I do not care if there is no depth or weight to them; they always possess charm, and they always keep to the point.'[17] What makes such intercourse pleasing is that it is the meeting of mature judgements seasoned with 'kindness, candour, gaiety and friendship'. It might be difficult to see how it can be an indifferent matter whether talented and rare interlocutors discuss their subjects without 'weight or depth', but the formulation is misleading. Earlier in the essay Montaigne apostrophises pedants who mask rather than illuminate their interests with long words and intellectual conceits.[18] Here he says that learning can only be part of the talk if it is not 'schoolmasterly, imperious and tiresome, as it usually is, but ready to take a lesson. We are only seeking to pass the time.'[19] The point, however, is that the value of talk with people chosen for their personal qualities is guaranteed by the latter: 'The mind of a well-bred person, familiar with the world of men, can be sufficiently agreeable in itself. Art is nothing else but the register and record of the works of such minds.'[20]

As a description of what friends should be and what friendship should yield, this is a more modest account than the more famous earlier one, to be discussed in a moment; it is presumably because Montaigne does not expect to experience such a friendship again, and therefore settles for a norm which is nevertheless good – this time, a case of not letting the best drive out the good. The unemphasised central point is the same as Plutarch's: choose the friend well, and the benefits of friendship follow: obvious, but no less persuasive for being so.

Still, the discussion ends on a melancholy note. The three relationships of the essay's title are friendships with men, sexual affairs with women (he says in passing, 'I would rather have beauty than goodness in my bed'), and love of books. Friendships are 'disappointingly rare'; love affairs 'wither with age'; the one true constant and comforting relationship is with one's books.[21] There follows a charming account of his library and its pleasures.

'Of Friendship' is a different and more intense work. It was originally written as a preface to a treatise by Etienne de La Boétie called *Discourse on the Voluntary Servitude* (or *The Protest*) which Montaigne planned to publish, but which appeared in print elsewhere before he could do so. It was used by Huguenots in their struggle for survival in the Wars of Religion then engulfing France. Although deeply sympathetic to the cause of religious peace, Montaigne – himself an outwardly observant Catholic but something of a sceptic within – did not wish to get embroiled in the quarrel. As a result he published the essay as a preface to a number of de La Boétie's poems instead.

De La Boétie's treatise does two things: it offers an analysis of how tyrants get and keep power, and it argues that real power is in the hands of the people, who can get it, without violence, if they will. As the work's title suggests, de La Boétie thought that, by accepting their servitude, the subjects of a tyrant were more at fault than the tyrant himself. In its time and context it was a work with potential to be inflammatory, and its adoption by the Huguenots as propaganda in their cause made it so. De La Boétie was himself Catholic, but in his work as a magistrate he had tirelessly striven to keep the peace between the religious factions, in his jurisdiction allocating churches or, where there was only one church in a village, different hours of worship to the different persuasions. When the edict of toleration for Huguenots was published in January 1571 he welcomed it joyfully.

Alas, de La Boétie was not long for the world. He fell ill and died at the young age of thirty-three, after he and Montaigne had enjoyed an intense and wonderful friendship for just four years. Montaigne, two years the younger, had also served as a magistrate, and they knew of one another long before they met. Montaigne had moreover read and greatly approved the *Voluntary Servitude* tract when it was circulating in manuscript 'among men of understanding'.[22] When they met it was as if they were predestined for friendship, so irresistibly were they drawn to each other, so immediate the attraction and understanding between them. 'At our first meeting, which happened by chance at a great feast and gathering in the city, we found ourselves so captivated, so familiar, so bound to each other, that from that time nothing was closer to either than each was to the other.'[23]

Despite the concord of interests and outlook, and the preparation their friendship had received from the fact that they knew of each other – and approved of what they knew – long before they met, Montaigne could only say, 'If anyone urge me to tell why I loved him, I feel it cannot be expressed but by answering: Because it was he, because it was myself.' He was emphatic in his view that

> [s]uch a friendship has no model but itself, and can only be compared to itself. It was not one special consideration, nor two, nor three, nor four, nor a thousand; it was some mysterious quintessence of all this mixture which possessed itself of my will, and led it to plunge and lose itself in his; which possessed itself of his whole will, and led it, with a similar hunger and a like impulse, to plunge and lose itself in mine. I may truly say *lose*, for it left us with nothing that was our own, nothing that was either his or mine.[24]

This beautiful and eloquent evocation of the psychological state they mutually felt they were in comes as close as anything can to the 'another self' ideal. Montaigne claimed that he felt complete certainty regarding his beloved friend's intentions and judgements, and that he could understand the motivations of any of his actions, because 'our souls travelled so unitedly together, they felt so strong an affection for one another, and with the same affection saw into the very depths of each other's hearts, that not only did I know his as well as my own, but I should certainly have trusted myself more freely to him than to myself.'[25]

Montaigne was convinced that everyday friendships could not be compared to this. Ordinary friendships are sustained by mutual help and kindnesses, but in so complete a union such considerations are irrelevant; for just as one cannot be said to be grateful for services one performs for oneself, or love oneself more for having performed them, so there was no question of anything implying 'separation and difference' between him and de La Boétie. Such words would include 'benefit, obligation, gratitude, request, thanks' – they simply did not apply.[26]

In preparation for describing this 'friendship so complete and perfect' Montaigne surveys the kinds of close relationships that might be supposed to rival it. First, it is natural to human beings to wish for the society of others. This is why Aristotle says that a statesman will be less interested in justice than in fostering ties of friendship, because a perfect society is one in which all are bound together by friendship. But the friendship has to be for its own sake, for relationships premised on the getting of pleasure, profit or some other advantage are less noble and fine – and in being less, are not properly friendships at all.[27]

Some might regard family relationships as comparable to the highest friendships, says Montaigne, but he disagrees; the sentiment of a child for its parents is one of respect, and cannot be friendship because friendship is nourished by 'familiar inter-course' requiring some equality of condition, age and knowl-edge, which by its nature the parent–child relationship lacks. Parents cannot confide their innermost thoughts to their chil-dren, and children cannot admonish their parents – admonition being among the first duty of friends, Montaigne says – so this even more emphatically rules friendship out of family relationships.[28]

The same is true of sibling bonds, for even though the 'name of brother is indeed a beautiful and affectionate one' there are many reasons (of inheritance, rivalry, conflict) which conspire to weaken that bond or break it. And anyway there is no obvious reason why the similarity and harmony required for the best kind of friendship should exist between brothers; it often happens that siblings and parents are very different from one another, and fail to get along as a result; that is a commonplace.[29]

And then there is the fact that family ties are obligatory impositions; they are not freely chosen on the basis of mutualities, but happen by accident. Our free will, on the contrary, 'produces nothing that is more properly its own than affection and friendship'.[30]

Montaigne does not think there can be friendship between men and women. Relationships between the sexes are 'carnal and subject to satiety', whereas friendship is increased by enjoyment, not satisfied by it, for it is not a physical but a spiritual thing.[31] He therefore also affects to frown on homosexual relations, the 'alternative permitted by the Greeks', but allows that when they occur in nobler hearts the relationship between a man and a boy could be salutary: the former can give the latter

> instruction in philosophy; lessons in religious reverence and in obedience to the laws; encouragement to die for the good of the country; examples of valour, wisdom, and justice, the lover studying how to make himself acceptable by the charm and beauty of his mind, that of his body having long ago faded, and hoping by this mental comradeship to make a stronger and more lasting union.[32]

The two parts of the account here are detachable. On the one hand what Montaigne says about his friendship with de La Boétie is moving and the finest rendering of what a friend's being 'another self' might actually involve. On the other hand there is little to accept in the rest of what he has to say. It is not clear that the best and highest kind of friendship is impossible across the sexes, nor that the bond of brothers cannot achieve that status, nor that as children grow up there cannot be friendship between them and their parents. Friendship need not displace other relationships, which is why lovers and siblings can be friends while still being lovers and siblings.

Moreover our contemporary sensibility finds the pederastic relation 'permitted by the Greeks' questionable for more grounds than the chief one. Do we want 'lessons in religious reverence and . . . encouragement to die for the good of the country'? Do we even want unquestioning 'obedience to the laws' when there might be grounds for changing some of them for better ones?

To say that the two parts of Montaigne's account are detachable is to say that it is unnecessary to the celebration of the kind of friendship he achieved with de La Boétie that other kinds of relationships, some of them involving friendship, have to be downgraded. This thought has a significant implication: that we might need a variety of relationships, not all of them friendships, and not all of our friendships necessarily of the highest quality and intensity, to live fully human lives. Montaigne described the immediate affection he and de La Boétie felt as inexplicable, but it is as surely the case that all relationships are prepared by antecedent experience, and that an explanation might be forthcoming from them. If so, it would include relationships which he compares unfavourably with the one they made possible.

Bacon remarks that the person who claimed that whoever delights in solitude must be either a god or a wild beast, managed thereby to pack a lot of truth and untruth together in very few words. For whereas a person who is averse to society indeed has something of the wild beast about him, there are those who seek solitude for reasons of meditation or self-improvement, and they are not gods but men; Bacon names some philosophers and hermits of the Church who fill the bill. But theirs is not real solitude just because they are not in the company of others. Real solitude is experienced by those who have no friends; for them the world is a wilderness.[33]

It might be commented here that by the phrase 'real solitude' Bacon means aloneness, and this, moreover, in the sense of loneliness; and this reminds us that we need to distinguish between solitude properly understood, which is generally the welcome physical absence of others, and loneliness, the unwelcome psychological absence of others (one can be very lonely in a crowd). In this sense solitude is a good, much needed on occasions, and loneliness invariably a bad thing for essentially social creatures such as humans are. Bacon's 'real solitude' should accordingly be construed as 'loneliness'; it is loneliness that makes the world a wilderness.

'A principal fruit of friendship,' says Bacon, 'is the ease and discharge of the fullness and swelling of the heart, which passions of all kinds do cause and induce.' The only medication for an oppressed heart is a friend, to whom one can 'impart griefs, joys, fears, hopes, suspicions, counsels' – rather like (he astutely observes) a non-religious 'shrift or confession'.[34] And he even notices how great monarchs, at some risk to their own security, are eager to have what the terminology of his own day denominated 'favourites' or 'privadoes', but which the Romans gave a more explanatory name: *participes curarum* – sharers in cares.[35] He cites examples of great Romans who, despite having extensive families, could not have the 'comfort of friendship' without someone to whom they were drawn and whom they had chosen to be such.[36] All of which proves, he says, the truth of the observation that those without friends are cannibals of their own hearts because they are unable to disburden themselves of what is in them.

So, says Bacon, the first great fruit of friendship is what it does for us emotionally, regarding our joys and griefs. The former are greater and last longer when we tell them to friends, and some of the burden of the latter is lifted when told to a sympathetic ear.[37]

The second fruit is as healthful for the intellect as the first is for the emotions. 'For friendship maketh indeed a fair day in the affections, from storm and tempests; but it maketh daylight in the understanding, out of darkness, and confusion of thoughts.' This is because by discussing ideas, marshalling thoughts, turning them into words, communicating them, 'he waxeth wiser than himself, and that more by an hour's discourse, than by a day's meditation'.[38] How true.

But this is the lesser benefit of two from this fruit of friendship; the first is getting wise counsel from someone who has your interests at heart and wishes you well. 'There is as much difference between the counsel that a friend giveth, and that a man giveth himself, as there is between the counsel of a friend, and a flatterer. For there is no such flatterer as is a man's self, and there is no such remedy against flattery of a man's self, than the liberty of a friend.' We might remonstrate with ourselves, we might read improving books of morality, but nothing compares to admonition delivered by someone who we know is concerned about us and desires to help.[39]

So: friendship's first fruit is 'peace in the affections'; the second is 'support of the judgement'; the last, 'like the pomegranate, full of many kernels', is the aid that friends give each other in many different ways in many different connections. It is to say far too little, Bacon asserts, to agree with the ancients that 'a friend is another self', because a friend is far more than himself. If a man has children, say, and dies, leaving them to the guardianship of a friend, then he is as it were living on in the friend and continuing his obligations to his children. If he is bodily confined somewhere, but needs to fetch or take something to another place, and his friend does it for him, then he has, as it were, two bodies. And so on: friends are more than another self because they multiply one into several selves by their aid.[40]

And there is more. How can a man speak of his own merits? They would 'blush in a man's own mouth' whereas they would sound gracefully in his friend's mouth. Again, a man might not be able to speak to his son but as a father, to his wife but as a husband, whereas his friend can speak to them as the case requires. 'To enumerate these things were endless,' says Bacon; 'I have given the rule, where a man cannot fitly play his own part; if he have not a friend, he may quit the stage.'[41]

There is all the merit of common sense and truth in these observations. The most notable thing about their tenor, in comparison to what is reported in foregoing pages, is their pragmatism and absence of high-flown sentiment or idealisation. And yet they catch the sense in which friendship is life-enhancing, by explaining succinctly and accurately how it is so. Perhaps Bacon wrote like this because he lived on the cusp of the time in which Renaissance turned into the dawn of science, a change to which he himself contributed.

If one were to choose a best account of friendship from the materials provided by these various sources so far, one that drew on Bacon and a de-theologised Augustine would recommend itself powerfully. They have the practicality, the real-world maturity, of thinkers who have lived as well as meditated on living; in their views one encounters experience and truth.

CHAPTER 6

From Enlightenment back to the Roman Republic

More slices of history, more labels: but as before, there is something definite captured by the labels, for the Enlightenment and the distinctive counter-movements it inspired are personalities in their own right, and ones that have made large differences to the course of history.

We would expect to find new elements in thinking about friendship in the Enlightenment, and indeed we do. What explains them is the change wrought by two major developments. The first is that the Enlightenment's leaders – meaning the thinkers and writers who articulated its new sensibility: Diderot, Voltaire, Hume, Kant and others – wished to apply the concepts and methods of natural science, as this had made such progress in the preceding century, to matters of society and human life. An empirical approach to enquiry, involving observation and the testing of evidence, and a discipline of reason shrived of 'Rationalist' elements which say that ultimate truths can only be ascertained by a priori means, constitute the method. Accordingly they place a new governor in the seat of authority over our minds and actions, supplanting tradition, dogma, the divine right of kings, revelation, ancient scriptures, pieties, or anything else that is not empirically derivable or testable, or which cannot survive the independent scrutiny of reason.

The second element follows from the first. It is that most of humanity had lived (and alas today still lives) under the falsehood that there is one great truth about everything, one and only one right answer to the question of how we should live: and that those in charge know what it is. Everyone must accept, conform and obey; failure to accept and obey carried very weighty punishments for most of history, the death penalty not the worst of them.[1] In contrast, the Enlightenment pointed to the existence of great diversity and plurality in human nature and talent, which shows that there are many more ways than one of making and living good lives.

The freedom to make choices consonant with one's own talents is indeed a precondition of good lives; and this freedom in turn requires freedom to think and act. Hence Kant's famous remark about *Aufklärung*, 'enlightenment', which incorporates both developments: 'Enlightenment is man's emergence from his self-imposed immaturity. Immaturity is the inability to use one's own understanding without another's guidance. This immaturity is self-imposed if its cause lies not in lack of understanding but in indecision and lack of courage to use one's own mind without another's guidance. *Sapere aude* (dare to know)! "Have the courage to use your own understanding," is therefore the motto of the enlightenment. Nothing is required for this enlightenment except freedom; and the freedom in question is the least harmful of all, namely the freedom to use reason publicly in all matters. But on all sides I hear: "Do not argue!" The officer says, "Do not argue, drill!" The tax man says, "Do not argue, pay!" The pastor says, "Do not argue, believe!" . . . We find restrictions on freedom everywhere. I reply: The public use of one's reason must always be free, and it alone can bring enlightenment to mankind.'[2]

Kant's own views on friendship underwent development as his philosophical position became more elaborate and fully worked out. In his early lectures on ethics (which consist of edited versions of his students' lecture notes) he regarded it as problematic to define friendship as arising from a concern to promote the happiness of others out of a general love for mankind, which is what morality asks of us. This is because 'anthropology' (meaning observation of human nature) does not suggest that human beings are naturally predisposed to 'confidence, cordial well-wishing and friendship', given that the primary motivation driving action is self-love, understood as the overriding interest in promoting one's own happiness.[3] So there appears to be a conflict. But Kant says that genuine friendship resolves the conflict by its mutuality: each will be interested in the other's happiness, each will nurture the other's welfare; 'the happiness of each is promoted by the generosity of others, and this is the Idea [*sic*, with a Platonic capital 'I'] of friendship, where self-love is swallowed up in the idea of generous mutual love.'[4]

But this is an idealisation, and in practice one cannot always rely on others to compensate for the neglect of one's own interests implicit in devotion to the interests of others. The ideal says this is how it should work, and the ideal is 'true and necessary' and it is what we ought to do from a moral point of view, even if from a 'natural' point of view it must be accepted that we will not do it. But we posit the ideal to ourselves because it is what gives us our sense of mankind's value.[5] There is a prefiguring here of the notion, fully developed in the 'Critical Philosophy' of Kant's later works, that we *must* make use of certain concepts in order to key a region of thought – for example, we *must* take it that we have a metaphysically free will, even though our empirical will is trapped in the mesh of causality, because otherwise we cannot make sense of moral agency and responsibility. The idea that the unattainable 'Idea' of friendship as complete mutuality of interest which trumps self-interest plays just such a role.

In these earlier thoughts on friendship Kant followed the Aristotelian division of kinds of friendship into those of need, taste and disposition. The first occurs when the parties 'entrust each other with reciprocal concern'.[6] The second is premised on the mutual pleasure taken in the association, and is typically expressed in courtesy or good manners; moreover it is more likely that the parties are attracted to each other more by their differences than by any similarities between them.[7]

The third kind of friendship is the highest, because it consists in a 'pure sincere disposition' of each towards the other. It rests on free and open-hearted communion, self-revelation and acceptance; each thereby has a friend 'in whom he can confide, and to whom he can pour out all his views and opinions; from whom he cannot and need not hide anything – with whom, in short, he is able to communicate fully'.[8]

In the later lectures on ethics Kant adds the idea that friendship requires equality in almost all respects, since without it there will be an aspect of the superior doing the inferior a favour by means of their friendship. But there is one respect in which there does not have to be equality, and that is in the degree to which one feels well-wishing love towards others. It does not have to be reciprocated, Kant says, because if reciprocation were necessary then it would not be possible for anyone to have a well-wishing attitude to mankind in general. However, when well-wishing is reciprocated by another person, the relationship turns into friendship; this is *amor bilateralis*.[9]

Kant's finished theory of friendship is found in his *Metaphysic of Morals*.[10] His definition of the 'general idea' of friendship is 'the union of two persons through equal mutual love and respect'. Love and respect operate differently in this union; love draws the two together, respect pushes them apart because by its nature it consists in there being a proper distance between them. 'This limitation upon intimacy,' he says, 'is expressed in the rule that even the best of friends should not make themselves too familiar with each other.'[11] As a result, true friendship is very hard to achieve; Kant quotes Aristotle's remark made in service of the same point: 'Friends, there is no such thing as a friend!' But it is 'a duty set by reason' to strive towards such friendship nonetheless. Kant's ethics in general is founded on the notion that duty – not inclination or affection or sentiment – is the sole ground of what is truly moral. In line with this austere deontology, he says that although the emotions engaged in friendship make it 'tender' they cannot be the ground for it, because they are too easily disrupted; the mutual liking and self-surrender have to be 'subjected to principles or rules preventing excessive familiarity and limiting mutual love by the requirement of respect'.[12] This requirement even qualifies how far the friends should go in the mutual disclosures of their confidential thoughts and feelings.[13]

'True friendship' – our 'no true Scotsman' is present again – is wearing a very stiff-collared Prussian uniform here, as does all of Kant's unbending ethics of duty. Elsewhere Kant says that one is not being moral if one plays with one's children out of affection or kindness, but only if one is doing it out of parental duty.[14] These are not very sympathetic views. Some have located their source in the strict and puritanical Pietistic version of Christianity in which Kant was brought up, though he was not a practising Pietist (or any kind of Christian, for that matter) in adult life; but a sense of unyielding duty can survive its origins.

A more likely reason, or pair of reasons, is that he disagreed with two fundamental tenets of David Hume's philosophy, one being that only emotion can be an impulse to action; the other being that our moral valuations spring from our emotional reactions, not from an objective source outside us.

On the first point Hume thought that if our 'passions' (our emotions) did not impel us to act, we never would, because no reason for doing something would ever seem compelling enough to override the opposing reason for not doing it. If we rely on reason to motivate us we would be in the position of Buridan's ass, which, standing between two bales of hay, died of starvation because it had no better reason to eat one than the other.[15]

The second point, relating to Hume's subjectivism regarding morals, is one's reaction to the loss of a law-giver as provided by religious tradition in the form of a suitably conceived deity. If moral principles and rules are not handed down from the sky, then what is the justification for saying that we must abide by them? Hume's optimistic answer is that the innate benevolence of human nature provides us with our morality. Kant could not agree, and sought the required objectivity in the rule of reason: the right thing to do is what reason tells us is the duty of anyone similarly placed.[16]

A less exigent view of the work done by reason in thinking about such ethical goods as friendship would allow it to recognise the importance – indeed the fundamental importance – of emotion in life. This is true of the emotions' role not just in our relationships, and in giving meaning, colour and flavour to our experiences, but even in our reasoning itself; as empirical work in psychology shows, emotionless reasoners are not good reasoners.[17]

The Enlightenment elsewhere has much less austere, far more human accounts to give of friendship. Voltaire's *Candide* might be a satire on the Leibnizian belief that this is the best of all possible worlds, but it is also an extended celebration of a variety of friendships, which Candide – by nature as by name – is so well disposed to form and maintain. The group of friends end up happily tending a garden in Istanbul after all their adventures, during which they stick together despite differences and difficulties. It is always interesting to inspect whether creators of fictional good companions had the capacity to be so themselves, and the thought occurs with Voltaire. People like Voltaire might lose as many friends as they make because of a too acidulous wit, but in his case there are proofs of high ability in this field; his friendship with Emilie du Châtelet was more than a 'mere' friendship for a time, but what principally underlay it was a meeting of minds and interests, an intellectual equality more powerful and interesting than anything else that could bind them together.[18]

There is no more direct statement of Voltaire's views on friendship than his poem 'The Temple of Friendship'. He imagines a plain little temple in a woodland retreat, dedicated to Friendship, where 'truth, simplicity and nature reign'. Few worship there, however, because hypocrisy, rivalry, betrayal, selfish ambition, petty differences that grow to great divisions, and envy destroy any chance people have of winning the prize that Friendship offers. What friendship is, then, is the reverse of these things: sincerity, co-operation, trust, concern for the other's interests, tolerance, mutual admiration and respect.

In his *Philosophical Dictionary* he writes,

Friendship is the marriage of the soul; and this marriage is subject to divorce. It is a tacit contract between two sensitive and virtuous persons. I say "sensitive," because a monk, a recluse can be not wicked and live without knowing what friendship is. I say "virtuous," because the wicked have only accomplices; voluptuaries have companions in debauch, self-seekers have partners, politicians get partisans; the generality of idle men have attachments; princes have courtiers; virtuous men alone have friends.

Not a great deal separates Voltaire's view of friendship from that of Cicero (in the *Philosophical Dictionary* entry he points out that Cicero had a friend – Atticus – which meant he was a virtuous man), and from Aristotle's view his own differs principally in not idealising friendship beyond the reach of most if not all people. But this difference is crucial. To take friendship out of the realm of idealisation into moral reality does it a service, something that arguably Kant fails to do.

Recognition of the difference between the contexts for discussing friendship in classical antiquity and the emerging industrial and commercial world of the eighteenth century helps to explain Adam Smith's views.[19] For him the resources for understanding personal relationships principally lie in facts about social organisation. Pastoral societies require extended families to stay together for 'common defence', whereas in commercial society where the rule of law will protect the least individual in the state, families disperse as each member seeks opportunities wherever his interests or talents take him.[20] Social relations therefore become more voluntary, and friendship emerges from the innate propensity people have to 'truck, barter and exchange'.[21] A similar idea occurs in Hume, who in an essay on trade remarks how commerce expands markets and trading activities, and therefore the range of acquaintances and friends that people acquire.[22] Commentators on both Smith and Hume notice the idea in both of 'cool' friendship – not in the sense of calculating, indifferent friendship, but neither – at the other end of the spectrum – the intense and personal bond to which the parties are happy to apply the term 'love', as in Montaigne's amazing mutuality, but something in between – something more like the respectful attachment that Kant, were he less formulaic, might applaud.

Two key Enlightenment ideas expressed in the views of Smith and Hume are progress and cosmopolitanism, and the latter partly helps to explain the idea of 'cool friendship': in a bigger and more diverse world the interactions of individuals who are no longer embedded in tight webs of family and community relationships – in village life, as Smith himself put it – might easily have a more transient and superficial quality. Another, connected, part of the explanation for this lies in the impersonal operation of markets and the increasing size of towns and cities where relationships are harder to form.

But this did not mean for Smith that friendship is doomed to become ever more instrumental and utilitarian, and more conditional on whether it is successfully both. On the contrary, he thought that once individuals escape from the obligation-imposing web of relationships which traditional societies throw around them, their friendships come to be more open, more freely chosen, based on sympathy and similarity of interests rather than instrumental necessity or prior commitment.[23] If that is the trade-off for the loss of traditional ties, themselves not always salutary, it looks like a good bargain.

Smith thought that commerce has a positive effect both on people and their relationships because it makes them more trust-worthy and punctual, at very least in their business dealings, because it is in their own interests to be so. But he had a worry too, which was that the new deracinated urban experience and the new patterns of working life could have ill effects, especially on morals and education, and on relationships themselves. He wrote that a man might have a character to lose in his country village because his behaviour would be constantly observed there, so he would have to mind himself; 'but as soon as he comes to a great city, he is sunk in obscurity and darkness. His conduct is observed and attended to by nobody, and he is there-fore likely to neglect himself, and to abandon himself to every low profligacy and vice.'[24] The remedy he suggested was that people should join a church so that others could help by keeping a watch on them. There is something bleakly Scottish and Presbyterian about this prescription, as there is in the pessimistic view of human nature that makes the solitary newcomer to town an inevitable catch for vice.

A man plays the part of a friend, says Smith, when he is generous from worthy motives, and thereby earns the good opinion of those he has treated well. To be 'in friendship and harmony with all mankind' as a result of deserving the favourable estimation of others is to be happy and at peace with oneself.[25] This, note, is a 'friendship to all'; the satisfactions that earlier theorists of friendship wished to achieve through more personal and intimate bonds Smith implies we can have in a tempered version of *agape*. No doubt, though, this way of being a friend also works at the personal level. Properly motivated generosity, if reciprocal, and reciprocally prompting 'favourable estimation', would be just the kind of cool friendship already described.

The idea of 'cool friendship' needs qualification in the case of Hume, though. He was famous for his sociability, nick-named 'le bon David' because of it; is that the extent of what he too meant? It would not seem so. 'Nothing touches a man of humanity more,' he wrote, 'than any instance of extraordinary delicacy in love or friendship, where a person is attentive to the smallest concerns of his friend, and is willing to sacrifice to them the most considerable interest of his own.'[26] Hume was an admirer of Cicero, and the idea of a 'man of humanity' is a Ciceronian version of the classical ideal of friendship.

A salient implication of these conceptions of friendship is that they are recognisably *humanist* in the contemporary meaning of the term, in the broad sense that they start from practical concerns of real people – not ideally virtuous or spiritually elevated agents – in the real circumstances of life, not in equally idealised circumstances where the cultivation of lofty virtues and the development of refined friendships can take precedence over the avocations of normal life.

Likewise the morality associated with these conceptions is secular and immanent, which is to say, humanistic too; this idea of a genuinely moral person is articulated by Henry Fielding – the morality of good-heartedness embodied in the characters of Tom Jones and Parson Adams. Tom, Fielding writes, had 'a kind and benevolent Disposition, which is gratified by contributing to the Happiness of others'.[27] The point is not to be morally perfect, but morally good. Tom has faults, of course, but as Mrs Miller tells Squire Allworthy (whose own name indicates a Fieldingesque ethical standing) even if Tom does not overcome them in time, 'they are vastly over-balanced by one of the most humane tender honest Hearts that ever Man was blest with'.[28] One of several implications is that such a person would be a good friend indeed, and two such people in relation would between them create a friendship such as friendship ought to be.

Good-heartedness is, of course, a close cousin of *benevolentia*; as this shows, the ancients and moderns do not differ by much in identifying the qualities indispensable to the possibility of friendship.

At the transition from the eighteenth to the nineteenth century – as it were with a combination of Enlightenment licence and Romantic zeal despite the sharp opposition of these outlooks, but with more of the latter so that one thinks of him as one of the first English Romantics – stands the extraordinary figure of William Godwin. No one has anatomised him and the impracticalities of his thought better than William Hazlitt, who knew him from childhood upwards and was much helped by Godwin's childlike benevolence. Hazlitt thought that Godwin had put morality above the reach of ordinary people by demanding 'universal benevolence' and a utopian dispensation as the theatre of its operation.[29] But there is more to Godwin than that, as his essay 'Of Love and Friendship' shows.[30]

Right at the beginning Godwin denies that equality is essential between friends. 'Who is it that says, "There is no love among equals?" Be it who it may, it is a saying universally known, and that is in every one's mouth. The contrary is precisely the truth, and is the great secret of every thing that is admirable in our moral nature.'[31] Love – of every kind: not just romantic or sexual love, but strong affection felt for another, as happens in friendship too – is not a 'calm, tranquil, and as it were half-pronounced feeling, but a passion of the mind'. It is not mere approbation of others, the kind of positive feeling one might have for acquaintances or clients, but a sentiment 'wherein the person in whom it resides most strongly sympathises with the joys and sorrows of another, desires his gratification, hopes for his welfare, and shrinks from the anticipation of his being injured; in a word, is the sentiment which has most of the spirit of sacrifice in it, and prepares the person in whom it dwells, to postpone his own advantage to the advantage of him who is the object of it'.[32]

Essential to this feeling is imagination. The cold light of scientific measurement, where everything is understood and reduced to a rule, is inimical to love, for the good reason that to love is to think of what is more absent than present, of things unseen rather than seen, of the future or the past rather than the present moment. 'Sentiment is nothing, till you have arrived at a mystery and a veil, something that is seen obscurely, that is just hinted at in the distance, that has neither certain colour nor outline, but that is left for the mind to fill up according to its pleasure and in the best manner it is able.'[33]

For Godwin the 'great model' of love in human beings is the 'sentiment which subsists between parents and children', and the charms even of sexual attraction and what Milton calls 'the rites mysterious of connubial love' are a function, Godwin claims, of the hope that they will produce offspring. Much of the essay is taken up with an examination of how the emotion of love is most fully expressed in this relationship. Given his view that love springs from 'the conscious feeling of the protector and the protected', and that it needs to be acted on – 'Our passions cannot subsist in lazy indolence; passion and action must operate on each other; passion must produce action, and action give strength to the tide of passion' – it is entirely natural to see the parent–child relationship as paradigmatic.[34] It is a view which does him warm credit, but it is implausible; by any standards the love of parents for children and its reciprocal are two very different kinds of feeling, and each is different again from the several other kinds of love there are. Godwin ignores the distinctions drawn by the Greeks between *agape, eros, ludus, storge, pragma* – respectively love for one's fellow humans, erotic love, playful love, companionate love, pragmatic love – and the combinations and different strengths of mixtures of these and perhaps yet others.

For our purposes the thesis is interesting when Godwin applies it to friendship as such. There too we find inequality the 'inseparable attendant' of perfect ties of affection.[35] He cites as the most celebrated instances of friendships those between Achilles and Patroclus, Orestes and Pylades, Aeneas and Achates, Cyrus and Araspes, Alexander and Hephaestion, and Scipio and Laelius. The parties to these relationships are, respectively, 'the true hero, the man of lofty ambition, the magnificent personage in whom is concentrated every thing that the historian or the poet was able to realise of excellence', on the one hand, and on the other 'the modest and unpretending individual in whom his confidence reposed'.[36] As Godwin sees it, the 'grand secret' of friendship is thereby revealed. It is that it consists in the repose of the loftier soul, its unbending or relaxation into the confidence and love of the inferior party. The greater party wishes to set aside the burden of greatness for a while, and be himself, relating to someone else 'as a man merely to a man'. He wishes to be sure that he is not being accosted with insincerity, flattered, adulated, fawned upon for gain or interest. 'What he seeks for, is a true friend, a being who sincerely loves, one who is attached to him, not for the accidents that attend him, but for what most strictly belongs to him, and of which he cannot be divested. In this friend there is neither interested intention nor rivalry.'[37]

But the inequality must not be too large; the inferior has to be able to comprehend the qualities of the superior, they must be able to discuss, to share attitudes and feelings about things, there must be confidence and trust between them; it will *seem* as if perfect equality subsists between them in their interaction, and this is premised on the understanding by both that

[t]here is in either party a perfect reliance, an idea of inequality with the most entire assurance that it can never

operate unworthily in the stronger party, or produce insincerity or servility in the weaker. There will in reality always
be some reserve, some shadow of fear between equals, which
in the friendship of unequals, if happily assorted, can find no
place. There is a pouring out of the heart on the one side, and
a cordial acceptance on the other, which words are inadequate to describe.[38]

Godwin is in one sense assuredly right in his analysis of the
friendships he cites; they were indeed friendships between
unequals; and in speaking exclusively of masculine friendships
Godwin is making his analysis turn on examples that could
only plausibly be masculine, even if there are relationships
between women that have the same inequality. But arguably the
inequality upon which Godwin focuses existed only in respect
of an external and perhaps superficial ranking of who and
what the men in his examples were. In the inner sanctum of
these relationships there had to be equality of a different and in
the end more fundamental sort – something indeed implicitly
acknowledged by Godwin himself in saying that the 'greater' of
the two needs a friend so that he can lay down the incum-
brances of station and be 'merely as man to man'. (And this is,
very persuasively, what one would take to be the case in friendships between women: that setting aside differences in status or
station would be precisely what allows the commonalities of
female experience to make and sustain the friendship that
ensues.) More to the point, the confidences and mutual understanding, the trust and shared knowledge and insight, without
which there could be no possibility of communion between

friends, require equalities of mind and character that are independent of social status or reputation.

Another implicit acknowledgement of this point, inconsistent with Godwin's main thesis, lies in his closing remarks, where he revisits the essential role of imagination in ties of affection. He there says,

> each party must feel that it stands in need of the other, and without the other cannot be complete; each party must be alike conscious of the power of receiving and conferring benefit; and there must be the anticipation of a distant future, that may every day enhance the good to be imparted and enjoyed, and cause the individuals thus united perpetually to become more sensible of the fortunate event which gave them to each other, and has thus entailed upon each a thousand advantages in which they could otherwise never have shared.[39]

It is hard to see this excellent description of what friendship requires of friends in any light other than that of equality, at least of an inward equality, which could alone make it possible.

And yet some of the examples we see in literature and legend have just the shape that Godwin argues is the right one for love in general and friendship in particular; not least the friendship of Achilles and his 'squire' Patroclus, described in the next chapter.

In the nineteenth century the theme of friendship takes a twist as a result of what in my opinion is a hitherto largely unnoticed connection: that as the European empires grew and came increasingly into conflict, leading directly and otherwise to the debacles of the twentieth century, the professionalisation of military and imperial service reawoke idealisations of Spartan hardiness and Roman Republican virtues, and with them the kind of men needed for demanding times – *men*, note: though some grand ladies of Rome are mentioned, and those Greek mothers who robustly told their sons to 'come home *with* their shields or *on* them', that is, victorious or dead. These trends have of course been noticed; what have been unnoticed are the models and examples cited in educating boys – specifically boys – destined to become District Commissioners in the jungle and cavalry officers at the head of a troop, in the duties of national and personal loyalty.

The Treaty of Westphalia in 1648, creating the Europe of nations which set the disastrous course towards nationalism and its discontents from which we still suffer, eventually required us to become patriots, as the Romans were. And therefore genera- tions of schoolboys were made to read (in Latin) about Mucius Scaevola putting his right hand into the flames to show that no matter how much Lars Porsena of Clusium tortured him, he would never betray Rome. We know with Dr Johnson that patri- otism is the 'last refuge of the scoundrel', but we still feel a tear welling up at *dulce et decorum est pro patria mori*, so thorough has the unconscious indoctrination been.

Tucked inside these confected sentiments, in novel after nineteenth-century novel of schooldays and imperial adven- tures and soldiering, and in cheap popular fiction about lads on the loose (forgotten now because not literary enough), are what in their own right are better matters: more and less direct, more and less po-faced and upstanding, dissertations on the ethos of friendship required for these Spartan and Roman Republican virtues. Examples are the two picaresque novels by Pierce Egan, *Life in London; or, The Day and Night Scenes of Jerry Hawthorn, Esq. and his elegant friend Corinthian Tom, accompanied by Bob Logic, The Oxonian, in their Rambles and Sprees through the Metropolis* (1820–21) and its sequel, *The Finish to the Adventures of Tom, Jerry and Logic in their Pursuits through Life in and out of London* (1827–28); Edward Bulwer-Lytton's *Paul Clifford* (1830), William Harrison Ainsworth's *Jack Sheppard* (1839), Thomas Hughes' *Tom Brown's Schooldays* (1857) and *Tom Brown at Oxford'* (1861), Disraeli's *Coningsby* (1844), the friendships in Dickens and Trollope, the virile comradeships in Buchan and Henty – the reading list is long, and to be complete it would have to include its tail reaching into the twentieth century to which – to cite a perhaps unexpected example – the Western ('cowboy') novel's trope of the hero and his sidekick belongs.[40]

Egan's trio of friends are rich and free to enjoy themselves, constituting a model for aspiring contemporaries and youths; the first of the two novels was a best-seller. Bulwer-Lytton's cheerful highwaymen heroes, Paul Clifford, Long Ned and Augustus Tomlinson, are three musketeers, though he himself likens them to Robin Hood's band. The group of men associated with Jack Sheppard are Jonathan Wild (these two are named for historical figures in the *Newgate Calendar* of criminals), Blueskin and Darrell, and between them they illustratively play out the nexuses of betrayal and loyalty around which nineteenth-century discussions of the hardy Roman-style concept of friendship revolved.[41]

Male friendship in the nineteenth century was the key to acceptance into masculine status by peers. Becoming a man lay in the gift of one's male friends after the *cursus honorarium* of life in boarding school or apprenticeship (both of which started very young); these all-male environments and their codes were formative, so it is inevitable that, in the way of those unconscious, undirected developments that so often look like conspiracies, a literature of direction should emerge, extolling the virtues (*vir*, remember, means 'man' in the sense of 'male', not 'humankind') required for, and warning against the vices attendant upon, masculine life.

Scarcely any discussion of male friendship in this or any period escapes speculation about the degree to which homosociality is in practice or in latency a form of homosexuality. Academic literary criticism naturally and inevitably pounces on the question, because anyone thinking about these matters naturally enough finds it hard to imagine psychological intimacy without the possibility that it might spill into physical intimacy. Of course, in the practice of our own lives we find little difficulty in resisting such spillage; it does not even seem to require resistance, for it is harder to cross the boundary between psychological and fuller forms of physical connection than otherwise. But presented with closeness between two people of any permutation of sexes, we automatically begin to wonder.

In the case of all-male upbringings in boarding schools or apprenticeships, and especially in the former, there is an institutional recognition that adolescent homosexuality occurs because of the unavailability of other outlets for the effect of raging hormones. As with homosexual practices in prisons, it is more often than not 'situational' and opportunistic (in America the phrase is 'gay for the stay'). The institutional recognition takes two forms: severe punishment if discovered, as a deterrent, and/or relentless scheduling from rising bell to lights out, filled with vigorous sports that leave no energy for sex.

It was a problem especially for the educational tradition that encouraged youths to take classical heroes as their models that there should be any ambiguity attaching to the question of friendship. In the Victorian public schools and two ancient universities, an expressly religious ideal of 'muscular Christianity' was proposed, and the propaganda against derogation from it was unequivocal. In *Tom Brown's Schooldays* Thomas Hughes leaves nothing to the imagination about what side we should be on, talking of a boy of suspect tendencies as 'one of the miserable pretty white-handed curly-headed boys, petted and pampered by some of the big fellows, who wrote their verses for them, taught them to drink and use bad language, and did all they could to spoil them for everything in this world and the next'.[42] Yet the intense friendships there and in the sequel, *Tom Brown at Oxford*, are couched in the language of sentiment and romance; at Oxford Tom makes the acquaintance of a manly Christian called Hardy, and is soon 'rapidly falling into friendship with Hardy. He was not bound hand and foot and carried away captive yet, but he was already getting deep into the toils.'[43]

The propaganda designed to deflect attention from *paederastia* and the sexual side of male friendships in the classical world was able to take a cue from Plato and generalise it:

That such friendships [as the heroic] in Greece and Rome existed with perfect purity of thought, and inspired a love of

fame and noble action, can hardly be doubted . . . the form
that love then so frequently took was in friendship, and there
aroused, as in its highest nature it always must, a desire for
all that is good and honourable in man.[44]

There is no reason to think that 'situational homosexuality'
does not occur outside the intense environment of boarding
school, given that almost all societies, even our much more
integrated contemporary Western society, still practise sexual
segregation of the young. But the question is whether these
considerations are pertinent to friendship as such. With what
frequency is it the case that if two men are close friends there is
something more to it than friendship? I address this question at
the end of the next chapter. At this juncture, though, it has to
be said that in the absence of public anxieties about homosexuality, and in line with the Romantic privileging of intense
emotions and sentiment, friendships between men were *allowed*
to be close and emotional, arm-in-arm, full of openly expressed
affection, and absorbing. The best proof of this is the photo-
graphic record, showing men hugging, holding hands, sitting
on one another's knees for the posed studio shot. Of course
some of the pictures might be of gay couples, but the likelihood
is that most were not; there are far too many of them, the poses
adopted by friends in front of the camera being intended as
visual records and expressions of their bond.[45]

What, though, is the ideal of friendship being expressed in
these treatments of it? It is a straight reprise not so much of the
classical ideal of the philosophers as of the classical example of
the heroes. In the jungle or on the battlefield, as on the sports
field, your friend is the one who will not let you down. He can be

trusted, relied upon. He will do the honourable thing. More, he will sacrifice himself for you; one recalls Sydney Carton doing a far, far better thing than he has ever done at the end of *A Tale of Two Cities*, and (in real life and death) Captain Oates leaving the tent in the Antarctic. He will 'play up and play the game' where you are concerned – and this therefore applies to you where he is concerned. Whatever other differences there are in rank or station, you are equals as friends. There need be no explicit contract of loyalty and service, because it is implicit in the very terms of friendship. If you wish to know how friends behave towards one another, you go to those classical sources, to the examples in legend and myth, and you do as friends did there.

As usual, the focus has been exclusively male so far, and that is because the theatre of friendship in this period was a public, external or outward one, and women were still enclosed in the domestic sphere, their relationships within it regarded as limited and shallow. That nothing could be further from the truth is obvious in the vastly richer and deeper analysis of relationships to be found in Jane Austen, the Brontës, George Eliot and Mrs Gaskell. It takes a single example to illustrate the point: the friendship between the two Bennet sisters Elizabeth and Jane in *Pride and Prejudice* (1813). Contrastingly, *Emma* (1816) explores how a woman can fail to be a good friend to another woman, as Emma's behaviour towards Harriet Smith and Miss Bates illustrates, and likewise with the set of contrasts between Frank Churchill, George Knightley, Mr Elton, Jane Fairfax, Mr Woodhouse and the rest.

What these novels show is that in Austen's ethics of friendship, the virtues of loyalty, love, steadfastness, frankness, honourable behaviour and truth are the overriding ones; a friendship is not merely premised upon but constituted of these, or it is not a friendship. It turns out that this is her ethics of love too, because she has little time for infatuation as a substitute; the love tie must be mature, considered and chosen; in short, marriage is a form of friendship (friendship with the addition of babies, you might say) and has to achieve that status at the outset if it is to be achieved at all.

Our own time finds this approach to love, though perhaps not to friendship, too cold and calculating. Conditioned by movies and romantic novels we think of 'relationships' in two categories. One is romance, which actually means infatuation, from which the question of sex is ineliminable, and which is thought to belong to early adulthood in the period before marriage (more accurately, a wedding) or a marriage-like settling down (more accurately, the decision to move in together), which is its natural terminus. Here all is intensity and breathlessness, longing, yearning, heartache and heart-break, soft-focus rosy scenes, tenderness, passion, desire, delight, and the correlative pains when things do not work out. In this relationship people are besotted by a crystal-covered false image of the other, as Stendhal says; they are in love with love, their bodies are responding to chemical messengers within and without and not to another human being; sex, longing and the dream are a thick opaque sheet between the lovers, who fondly imagine they are closer to each other and mutually more intimately known and knowing than with anyone else ever.[46]

Jane Austen thought infatuation irresponsible, and the ancient Greeks thought it the cursed mischievousness of Cupid with his arrows, against which none, not even the gods themselves, are proof.

The other category is marriage or marriage-like settling-down, with children and a mortgage in many cases; and the discussion of this relates to its challenges and problems, its failures, how to keep the sex going, how to cope with the infidelity that the artificialities of monogamy prompt, and so on. Here, if one or more of habit, compromise, affection and kindness have not made a peace, all is effort ('one has to work at a marriage') and even struggle, with discussion, emotional negotiations, concessions, silences, quarrels, perhaps marriage counsellors, too often lawyers – and then perhaps Dr Johnson's triumph of hope over experience, though often the second or subsequent attempts have more of the character Jane Austen would approve, than the allure of ignorance on whose basis the first attempt was made.[47]

Homosexual relationships of the cottaging variety stand, with certain others, outside these categories, though perhaps closer to the first; but it is interesting to note how, as this sexuality becomes ever more accepted and mainstream, many gays themselves wish to conform to the heterosexual norms, including marriage and family life.[48]

If nothing else is shown by the modern forms of relationship that see 'love and marriage' as higher goals than friendship, contrasting with the belief through most of history that frienship is the highest form of human relationship, it is that we have a less clear idea than our forebears had of what friendship is. Perhaps this is not just because it is less important than 'love and marriage'-type relationships now are; perhaps it is because it now takes so many more forms.

PART II

Legends

CHAPTER 7

Excursus: Friendship Illustrated

There have been many references to legendary friendships, fictional and otherwise, in the foregoing pages. It is of central interest to know what those who cited them intended to illustrate by their means. The assumption made in the references to them was that if you wish to know what a friend is, what friendship is, how friends behave towards one another, you go to the classical examples and learn from them.

The first two examples in the world's formative literature, standing as the pillars of the gate into this subject, are Achilles and Patroclus, and David and Jonathan. Both pairs introduce the immediate difficulty, discussed more fully at the end of this chapter, that so many of the classical examples seem to be homoerotic loves as well as – or differently from? – friendships. There are very few examples of woman–woman friendships in this category, or man–woman friendships. In the latter case the exceedingly few outstanding relationships of the kind that existed between Pericles and Aspasia also had other dimensions, and some would doubtless argue that perhaps they were those dimensions more than they were friendships as such; but that would be to beg the question against the thought that such relationships could be both friendships and sexual loves, which the characters and intellects of both Pericles and Aspasia strongly suggest.[1]

Let us begin with the first of the first: the relationship between two Greek warriors, one of whom was the beautiful and all but invincible young hero whose quarrel with Agamemnon is the starting point for Homer's *Iliad*.

Homer does not say that the two were lovers. In fact he seems to suggest otherwise; in Book IX when the two go to bed after being visited by Odysseus and Ajax, Achilles sleeps on one side of an inner room with 'beside him the daughter of Phorbas, lovely Diomede, whom he had carried off from Lesbos', while Patroclus 'lay on the other side of the room, and with him fair Iphis whom Achilles had given him when he took Scyros the city of Enyeus'.[2]

This heterosexual arrangement is clear enough. But what would hearers of the Homeric poems in the ancient Greek world, and later – after they were collected and written down at the behest of Peisistratus – their then readers, have assumed about them? The answer is that they did indeed assume that they were lovers also; for this we have the authority of Aeschylus in fragments from his lost play *The Myrmidons*, Plato in the *Symposium*, and Aeschines' *Timarchus* among others.[3] And there was a frisson of disapproval about them on the part of some ancients, because although Achilles was the younger, or thought to be so – in ancient depictions on vases and the like he appears without a beard while Patroclus has one – he was regarded as the lover, playing the part of the *erastes*, and

Patroclus the beloved, thus playing the part of the *eromenos*. This upsets the right order in several ways: the *erastes* was meant to be a bearded man, the *eromenos* a beardless boy, usually taken to be between twelve (the lowest legal age for this in ancient Athens) and about seventeen, when too much body hair was becoming visible.

Aeschylus is responsible for nominating Achilles as the *erastes*, prompting Phaedrus in Plato's *Symposium* to disagree, arguing that he must have been the *eromenos* on the grounds of his beardlessness. In his own *Symposium* Xenophon has Socrates say that Achilles and Patroclus were not lovers, giving no indication to that effect in the *Iliad*, to which Aeschines later responded by saying that any educated person could read between the lines to see what the true state of affairs was.

It has been pointed out that the tradition of *paederastia* – love between men and boys – was of much later date than the Trojan War period, whenever that date was, in which case there is considerable anachronism here. If there was no such tradition at the time, the social superiority of Achilles to Patroclus might in any case have made its own material difference to who was, so to speak, on top in this aspect of the relationship if there were one such. Other scholars, however, say that pederastic relationships were common and widespread throughout prehistorical Europe as an important part of social structure.

Possibly though, the identification of Achilles' and Patroclus' respective ages is a mistake; in the scene in Book I where Athena materialises beside Achilles to prevent him from drawing his sword on Agamemnon (because of their quarrel over the slave girl Briseis), Homer describes Achilles' chest as 'shaggy', which suggests maturity; although he also describes his hair as 'yellow', which suggests youth in so far as blond hair tends to darken with the years.

The evidence either way is not definitive, though the time and its traditions would make perfectly plausible the claim that the two were or had been lovers too, or were simply not bothered by any supposed difference between the two statuses. But we are emphatically shown, not just told, how very close they were as friends: to sleep in the same room each with his own concubine suggests great mutual ease.

There does however seem to be a good deal of Godwin's inequality in the relationship. When the heralds come, in Book I, to take Briseis away from Achilles for Agamemnon, it is Patroclus who does his 'dear friend's' bidding to fetch her out of the tent and hand her over. In Book IX, when Odysseus and Ajax go to plead with Achilles to rejoin the battle because the Trojans are gaining the upper hand, Achilles instructs Patroclus to set out a bowl and mix the wine and water for the guests. 'Patroclus did as his comrade bade him,' Homer tells us; and then Patroclus proceeded to cook dinner for them all, mending the fire and roasting loin of sheep and goat and 'the chine of a fat hog' on it. Achilles carved and Patroclus handed the meat round on bread; Achilles then told Patroclus to offer sacrifice to the gods, after which they all fell to eating.

Despite the best efforts of the visitors to persuade him to relent, Achilles refused, so after dinner they left. Aged Phoenix remained to stay the night, so Achilles told Patroclus to arrange a bed for him. Acting as steward, Patroclus ordered the slaves to lay out a mattress covered with fine linens for the old man.

All this shows that Patroclus was in a servitor's role, even though he is Achilles' 'dear friend', as Homer puts it. The impression of inequality is reinforced in Book XVII when Patroclus is described as Achilles' 'squire'. In Book XI, when Achilles sees from the stern of his ship how badly the battle is going for the Greeks, he calls Patroclus and tells him that he saw old Nestor carrying a wounded man back to camp, and instructs him to find out who it is. Patroclus runs to ask; Nestor invites him in but Patroclus says, 'Noble sir, I may not stay, you cannot persuade me to come in; he that sent me is not one to be trifled with . . . I see who has been wounded; I must go back and tell Achilles, you know what a terrible man he is, and how ready to blame where no blame should lie.'[4] This does not sound too good; Patroclus is scared of Achilles' wrath; the relationship now appears more unequal than even Godwin would approve.

Nevertheless Patroclus welcomes Nestor's suggestion that he should put on Achilles' armour and lead out the Myrmidons, and sets off to return. On the way he sees another friend, Eurypylus, staggering from the battle with an arrow in his thigh, and stops to help him. He is still with Eurypylus, 'entertaining him with his conversation and spreading herbs on his thigh to ease the pain', when the Trojans breach the Achaeans' long wall and advance towards the ships. Seeing the mortal danger of the Greek host, Patroclus leaps up; 'I know you want me now,' he says to Eurypylus, 'but I cannot stay longer, for there is hard fighting going on; a servant will care for you now. I must hasten to Achilles, and make him fight if I can; maybe the gods will help me to persuade him. A man does well to listen to a friend.'[5]

The Trojans were getting perilously close to setting fire to the Greek ships when Patroclus ran up to Achilles, weeping for the fate of his fellows. 'When Achilles saw him thus weeping he was sorry for him and said, "Why, Patroclus, do you weep like a silly child who comes running to its mother and begs to be taken up and carried?"' Patroclus answers,

I weep for the disaster that is befalling our Argives; all our champions are lying wounded at their ships . . . O Achilles – so inexorable? May it never be my lot to nurse a passion such as you have done, to the harm of your own good name! Who in future will speak of you unless you save the Argives now? You know no pity; Peleus was not your father or Thetis your mother, but instead the grey sea and the sheer cliffs are your parents, so cruel and remorseless are you . . . At least send the Myrmidons with me; let me wear your armour; the Trojans may mistake me for you and therefore quit the field, giving the hard-pressed Achaeans some breathing time.[6]

Achilles was 'deeply moved' by this straight talking, such as one friend might well address to another. Although unable to relent in his anger against Agamemnon, he fatefully agreed to Patroclus' suggestion. While Patroclus put on the personating armour Achilles went through the camp rousing his troops. The Myrmidons then swarmed out of their camp like wasps, Patroclus calling to them 'at the top of his voice, '"Myrmidons, followers of Achilles son of Peleus, be men, my friends, fight with might, that we may win glory for the son of Peleus, who is far the foremost man at the ships of the Argives – he, and his fighting followers. . ."'[7] The sight of them threw the Trojans into confusion. They fought hard in retreat; Patroclus drove his chariot into all the thickest parts of the fighting, cutting off the

Trojan battalions as they tried to escape, doing terrible slaughter among them right up to the walls of Troy, which he would have attacked had the god Apollo himself not warned him off on the grounds that it was not his destiny.[8]

It was also Apollo, carrying out the decrees of fate, who undid Patroclus after the latter's mighty acts. He struck Patroclus a blow on the back, between the shoulder blades, that dazed him, and before he could clear his head one of the Trojans thrust a spear into his back, and Hector drove another into his belly, pulling it out by placing his foot on Patroclus' chest, and then claiming his armour – the armour of Achilles.[9] For the rest of the day the battle raged around Patroclus' corpse, each side trying to claim the body of 'the squire of the fleet son of Peleus'.[10]

With Patroclus dead the Trojans again began to get the upper hand. A messenger, Antilochus, was sent to Achilles to tell him of Patroclus' death, which however Achilles had already begun to fear because he could see the Greeks being driven back towards their ships again.[11] Confirmation had the inevitable effect.

A dark cloud of grief fell upon Achilles as he listened to Antilochus. He filled both hands with dust from the ground, and poured it over his head, disfiguring his comely face, and letting the refuse settle over his shirt so fair and new. He flung his huge length down at full stretch, and tore his hair with his hands. The bondswomen whom Achilles and Patroclus had captured screamed aloud for grief, beating their breasts, their limbs failing them for sorrow. Antilochus bent over Achilles the while, weeping and holding both his hands as he lay groaning, for fear that he might stab himself. Then Achilles gave a loud cry and his mother heard him as she was sitting in the depths of the sea at the side of the Old Man her father, whereon she too screamed, and all the goddess daughters of Nereus that dwelt at the bottom of the sea came gathering round her.[12]

Achilles' grief is not just for the loss of his friend, but for his failure in not being by his side to protect him. 'Said Achilles in his great grief, "I would die here and now, in that I could not save my comrade. He has fallen far from home, and in his hour of need my hand was not there to help him." '[13]

Achilles' mother, silver-footed Thetis, arranged to have a new set of armour made for him by Hephaestus. He had to wait for it until the next day before he could set out to take revenge on Hector. But to give the Greeks heart he mounted the defensive trench by the wall, and three times shouted, which sent panic among the Trojans, and heart into the Greeks, who were at last able to drive Hector off the body of Patroclus and bring it back to Achilles.[14]

All night long the Myrmidons gathered with Achilles around the bier of Patroclus where it was laid after they had 'washed off the clotted gore'. The next day, wearing the beautiful armour made for him by the god, Achilles went to battle, killing many and driving the rest behind their city's walls; and at last killing Hector himself, whose body, in his grief and rage, he dishonoured by dragging it three times round the walls of Troy behind his chariot.[15]

That night Patroclus came to him in a dream, saying,

'Let not my bones be laid apart from yours, Achilles, but with them; even as we were brought up together in your own home, what time Menoetius brought me to you as a child from Opoeis . . . your father Peleus took me into his house, entreated me kindly, and named me to be your squire; therefore let our bones lie together in a single urn, the two-handled golden vase given to you by your mother.' Achilles answered, 'Why, true heart, I will do all as you ask. Draw closer to me, let us once more throw our arms around one another, and find sad comfort in the sharing of our sorrows.' He opened his arms towards him as he spoke and would have clasped him, but there was nothing, and the spirit vanished as a vapour . . . Achilles sprang to his feet, smote his two hands together, and made lamentation.[16]

After the funeral and the games that followed, in which Achilles gave prizes to the victors, there was a feast, and everyone went to sleep;

but Achilles still wept for thinking of his dear comrade, and sleep, before whom all things bow, could take no hold upon him. He turned this way and that as he yearned after the might and manfulness of Patroclus; he thought of all they had done together, and all they had gone through both on the field of battle and on the waves of the weary sea. As he dwelt on these things he wept bitterly and lay now on his side, now on his back, now face downwards, till at last he rose and went out as one distraught to wander upon the seashore. Then, when he saw dawn breaking over beach and sea, he yoked his horses to his chariot, and bound the body of Hector behind it that he might drag it about. Thrice did he drag it round the tomb of Patroclus, and then went back into his tent, leaving the body on the ground full length and with its face downwards.[17]

The relationship between Patroclus and Achilles is a Godwinian friendship, sure enough, in the inequality of status and station between the two; but contemplating it makes one think that it is so because of the antecedent condition of the parties to it in the sense that it is not a *friendship* because one of the parties is the natural or social superior of the other, as Godwin would have it, but rather it is a *Godwinian* friendship because one is the natural or social superior of the other. Achilles was a king, Hamlet was a prince, so Achilles' relationship with Patroclus, as Hamlet's with Horatio, as Prince Hal's with Falstaff, is conditioned by the antecedent fact of rank. People do not become friends *because* one has some form of superiority over the other, unless it is a friendship instituted by the inferior for his gain or advancement, which we do not think is genuine friendship at all; on the contrary, it would seem that there has to be a sharing of outlook and interests, and near-equality of abilities and moral nature, for any two or more people to bond, sometimes *in spite of* other reasons – those selfsame social reasons, and other differences of natural endowment – that might keep them apart.

The questions that arise with Achilles and Patroclus also arise with David and Jonathan in the first book of Samuel in the

Tanach (the work that Christians call the Old Testament). Biblical stories have an arbitrariness of narrative direction variously altered, explained, justified and glossed by the convenient interventions of a deity – and the deity's equally convenient absences at other times – which masks their oddity. In the story told in Samuel Book I we have simply to take the following as background: the first king of united Israel is Saul, who as a young man had been out looking for his father's donkeys one day when Samuel saw him and, prompted by God, chose him to be king. But God came to regret the choice of Saul because of his disobedience; ordered to massacre all the Amalekite men, women, children and livestock, Saul chose to keep the best livestock and the Amalekite king Agag alive. When Samuel remonstrated with him on God's behalf, Saul had Agag brought to him, and chopped him up into small pieces.[18]

This was not enough to reconcile God and Samuel to Saul, so God sent Samuel to anoint the person whom he had identified among the sons of Jesse in Bethlehem to be the next king of Israel. This was David.[19] Saul's abandonment by God resulted in an evil spirit tormenting him, and he needed comfort; someone had spotted how well David played the lyre, and as he was accomplished in other ways too, he was recommended to the king. When David played the lyre it refreshed the king and the evil spirit left him alone. Saul therefore kept David with him.[20]

At that time Israel was at perpetual war with the Philistines, who had stolen the Ark of the Covenant. As the two armies were facing one another across a valley between Elah and Socoh one day, the Philistines' champion, Goliath the giant, issued a challenge to single combat. David responded, and stepped forward armed only with a sling and five smooth stones, provoking Goliath's contempt. He only needed one of the stones; it sank into the giant's forehead and killed him.[21]

While Saul was commending David after this incident, Saul's son Jonathan, standing by, seems to have fallen instantly in love with him. 'As soon as he had finished speaking to Saul, the soul of Jonathan was knit to the soul of David, and Jonathan loved him as his own soul. And Saul took David that day and would not let him return to his father's house. Then Jonathan made a covenant with David, because he loved him as his own soul. And Jonathan stripped himself of the robe that was on him and gave it to David, and his armour, and even his sword and his bow and his belt.'[22]

Saul put David in command of his army, and David was immensely successful. David married Saul's daughter Michal. When the women of Israel sang 'Saul has killed his thousands, and David his tens of thousands', jealousy rose in Saul's breast against David, and he plotted to put an end to him by sending him on a dangerous mission: to get a hundred Philistine foreskins. David brought back two hundred.[23]

Saul resolved to have his son Jonathan and his servants kill David. But because he 'delighted' in David, Jonathan warned him of his danger, and then succeeded in dissuading Saul – but only temporarily, for soon thereafter Saul himself attempted to kill David by hurling a spear at him; and when David fled, set agents to watch his house in order to catch and kill him.[24]

All this time David benefited from Jonathan's protection and help. Saul's anger was kindled against Jonathan because of this:

You son of a perverse, rebellious woman, do I not know that you have chosen the son of Jesse to your own shame, and to the shame of your mother's nakedness? For as long as the son of Jesse lives on the earth, neither you nor your kingdom shall be established. Therefore send and bring him to me, for he shall surely die. Then Jonathan answered Saul his father, 'Why should he be put to death? What has he done?' But Saul hurled his spear at him to strike him. So Jonathan knew that his father was determined to put David to death. And Jonathan rose from the table in fierce anger and ate no food the second day of the month, for he was grieved for David, because his father had disgraced him.[25]

When the friends met in a secret place soon afterwards 'they kissed one another and wept with one another, David weeping the most. Then Jonathan said to David, "Go in peace, because we have sworn both of us in the name of the Lord, saying, 'The Lord shall be between me and you, and between my offspring and your offspring, forever.'"'[26]

Saul and Jonathan died in the wars against the Philistines – Saul voluntarily, falling on his sword to avoid capture – prompting a lamentation from David which includes the moving verses: 'Jonathan lies slain on your high places; I am distressed for you, my brother Jonathan; very pleasant have you been to me; your love to me was extraordinary, surpassing the love of women. How the mighty have fallen, and the weapons of war perished!'[27]

The verses are few in which the relationship of Jonathan and David is described, but a mighty edifice has been erected on them. There are immediately recognisable features: one is the instant liking that Jonathan took to David, exemplifying the point so frequently made that the affinities of the best kinds of friendship are natural and spontaneous. Another is the intensity of the bond; it 'surpasses the love of women'. They kiss and embrace. Even though Jonathan is a prince, the son of a king, and David a commoner, it is Jonathan who defers to David, telling him that he will be at David's side when the latter rules over Israel; Jonathan is David's social superior but inferior in quality and destiny, which seems to balance out. They were 'very pleasant' to each other, they loved each other, and with a love surpassing that of women: the avowal to that effect is a passionate one, whether homosocial or homosexual.

The biblical account compresses and distorts time in such a way that one does not know how much of it the two spent together, nor their respective ages. They were brothers-in-law as a result of David's marriage to Jonathan's sister Michal, and it is possible to imagine that there were periods of time when they all lived in the same city, and when the two men went to war together, before Saul's jealous madness made David a fugitive. But that is surmise merely, on the basis of the slender evidence.

On this same slender evidence the debate takes familiar contours. Rabbinic commentators use it to illustrate the enduring nature of unselfish love, as contrasted with the inconstancy of love founded on utility or interest only. Christian writers wish to see the relationship as platonic, an inevitable choice given that it belongs to a tradition which sees the overtly erotic Song of Solomon as an allegory for God's love of the Church.[28] But by the medieval and Renaissance periods others were thinking differently. The openly homosexual love of Edward II and Piers Gaveston was expressly likened in near-contemporary accounts to the love between Jonathan and David and Achilles and Patroclus.[29] In the *Annals* of Roger of Hoveden the relationship between Philip II of France and Richard I of England (the 'Lionheart') invited the same comparisons in being described thus: 'Richard Duke of Aquitaine [later Richard I], the King of England's son, stayed with Philip King of France, who so much honoured him for a long time that they ate at the same table every day from the same dish, and at night were not in separate beds. The French king loved him as his own soul, and so much did they love each other that the King of England was amazed by it and marvelled at it.'[30] This amity did not last; the two went to war against each other later.

That this was a homosexual affair and not merely an intense friendship is suggested by Roger's report, further on in the *Annals*, that when Richard was king he was harangued by a hermit warning him of the punishment suffered by Sodom and telling him, ' "Abstain from what is unlawful, for if you do not, the vengeance of God will overtake you." But the King, intent on the things of this world and not those of God, was not so readily able to withdraw his mind from unlawful things.'[31]

Interpretations of the relationship between Jonathan and David that see it as expressly homoerotic are very naturally offered by gay men, of course; the beautiful and influential depictions of David by Donatello and Michelangelo are cases in point. Their legitimacy has much to do with the fact that David is described in the Bible as handsome, and it is natural to think that when physical beauty is part of the reason for one person's attraction to another, it adds to the interest of the attractor's personality. Jonathan's liking for David is instantaneous, which is of a piece with the sexually based interest immediately felt when people are attracted by one another's looks in the ordinary course of life.

On the other hand, the Jewish tradition was emphatically against homosexuality, and the penalties for it were harsh. David and Jonathan had wives and concubines and children, so it is perfectly possible that they might both have been straight men, and the love they felt for each other which 'surpassed the love of women' might have been a purely intellectual and emotional one – which is to say: friendship as such, friendship in the most straightforward sense. Or there is yet another interpretation, one that might apply to many non-sexual close relationships between men which might have been given physical expression in more favourable circumstances, but might not even have been fully realised as sexual by the parties themselves; and which precisely for that reason were intense, loyal and consuming, but again amounted to friendships in the simplest sense of the term even with the unexpressed implications as a given.

The best-known story from ancient literature that contains an account of devoted friendship between women is the Bible's Book of Ruth. In its opening chapter it tells of how a widow, Naomi, whose husband and two sons have died, leaving her with her daughters-in-law, decides to return to her homeland of Judah, and tells the daughters-in-law to go home to their own families because, being too old, she will have no more sons for them. 'Go back, each of you, to your mother's home. May the Lord show you kindness, as you have shown kindness to your dead husbands and to me. May the Lord grant that you will find peace in the home of another husband. Then she kissed them goodbye and they wept aloud.'[32]

One of them, named Orpah, does as she is bidden; the other, Ruth, 'clung to her' and refused to go: 'Do not urge me to leave you or to turn back from you. Where you will go I will go, and where you stay I will stay. Your people will be my people and your God will be my God. Where you die I will die, and there will I be buried. May the lord deal with me severely if even death separates you and me.'[33] Things turn out well for the two women in Judah, where Naomi helps Ruth get a kind new husband, by whom she has a son, Obed, who is the father of Jesse, who is the mother of David.

The story is, as usual, multiply appropriated; it is a text for Jewish converts, which Ruth was, and for lesbians, and for those who have moral points to make about women or daughters-in-law, and for those who see allegory everywhere. Scholars point to the possibility of a very late composition of the story, which has all the marks of a novella perhaps composed in Hellenistic times.[34] The characters' names have meanings suited to the story; 'Naomi' means 'gracious one' but she asks to be called 'Mara' after her bereavements, for it means 'the bitter one'. 'Ruth' means 'friend'. The other names work likewise.

This is a story about friendship, straightforwardly so, despite the best efforts of those who claim that a lesbian relationship is proved by the fact that the word 'love' in 'Ruth loved Naomi' is the same 'love' as is used in Genesis in saying 'Adam loved Eve' – that is, conjugal or sexual love, 'how spouses are supposed to feel for each other'.[35] It would be to the good if such an infer- ence were otherwise supported, but it is not. What the Book of

Ruth seems to offer is something every bit as good: an example of friendship across generations, and as it happens across a cultural divide too, given that Ruth was not Jewish by origin. Ruth's reluctance to part from Naomi demonstrates her attachment, but the words of Naomi to her daughters-in-law, and the kissing and weeping that attended them, show the attachment to be mutual. There is however no discussion of the nature or source of the feelings involved; they are just there to be taken for granted.

We are anecdotally familiar with the historical fact, no less comfortable now for being one, that most women's lives have been segregated ones lived mainly in circumscribed domestic spheres. Within them all their relationships took shape; chiefly with other women and children, and in more limited and defined ways with one or a very few men. Anecdote also tells us that hostilities between women can be bitter, but that the comradeship of a shared and often difficult lot was a powerful and strengthening fact too. Ruth and Naomi represent two women on their own, travelling, having to make their way in circumstances inimical to independent women – in fact their salvation lies in Ruth's being able to remarry. That their society provided protection for women against being left outside the ambit of help does it credit, but the better point of the story is that the friendship of the two women is the basis for overcoming the difficulty they were in.

A second Homeric pair quoted as a model for friendship is Diomedes and Sthenelus. Diomedes is a victim of editing; some say that the account of his prowess and deeds in Books V and VI of the *Iliad* was once a separate poem in his honour, and he was indeed much cited in ancient times, admired, accorded eventual divine status, and claimed as the founder of many cities. But when the poem was edited into the body of the *Iliad* he lost the salience it gave him. Even then, he is described there as second only to Achilles in valour and fighting ability, and unlike Achilles he retains his nobility of bearing throughout. He was friendly with Odysseus, like whom he had a sharp mind, and he was one of those who hid in the belly of the Wooden Horse to overcome Troy at last.

Diomedes began as one of the Seven Against Thebes, and was a suitor of beautiful Helen. Her suitors made an arrangement among themselves that whoever won her hand would have the support and protection of the others should anything happen. Diomedes was accordingly bound to help Menelaus after the rape of Helen.

Everywhere there is Diomedes, there is Sthenelus. They were side by side as two of the Seven Against Thebes, they were both in the belly of the Wooden Horse. When Diomedes is struck by an arrow in the shoulder during fierce fighting in Book V of the *Iliad*, Sthenelus pulls it out. Afterwards, as two mighty warriors of the Trojan force are rushing at them, he says to Diomedes, 'Diomed, son of Tydeus, man after my own heart, let's get out of here.' (Diomedes refuses, on the grounds that he never runs away from danger.) When Agamemnon criticises the pair, Diomedes remains calm but Sthenelus gets very cross. In Book IX, addressing the Greek host which is contemplating packing up and leaving, Diomedes says that even if the rest of them go, he and Sthenelus will stay and fight until the towers of Troy fall.

The interest attaching to Diomedes and Sthenelus is that they figure in the twenty-second of the *Private Orations* of

Themistius, a philosopher and statesman who lived in fourth century CE Constantinople. The essay, written in Greek , is entitled 'On Friendship'. The warrior pair is cited with others, including Achilles and Patroclus, who are bonded together because in Themistius' view they make contrasting pairs. 'Homer, you know, knew how to depict friendship as well as war,' he wrote. 'He represented Patroclus as Achilles' friend, gentle Patroclus and pompous Achilles. He also wrote about Sthenelus and Diomedes, the latter long-suffering and the other unable to bear any insolence.' Homer gives evidence of this in Book IV of the *Iliad* where Agamemnon chides Diomedes and Sthenelus for not being quicker to join in the battle, as their fathers would have done. Diomedes is embarrassed by this, and keeps quiet, but Sthenelus is very annoyed: 'Don't lie, son of Atreus, given that you can speak truth if you want to! We regard ourselves as better men than our fathers, for we captured seven-gated Thebes, though the walls were thicker and our men fewer in number than when our fathers tried, whereas they died in that earlier attempt.' At this Diomedes chides him in his turn: 'Diomed looked sternly at him and said, "Hold your peace, my friend, as I bid you. It is not wrong for Agamemnon to urge us on, for victory will be to his glory, and defeat to his shame. Let us ago, and acquit ourselves with valour!"'[36]

The oration on friendship advises on how to choose a friend, and how to keep him once got.[37] Themistius describes himself as a devotee of 'true and sincere friendship', and would rather have one such 'than a Nisean horse, a Celtic hound, Darius's gold, the bull in Crete, or Achilles' shield'.[38] He has therefore given much thought to how one finds really good friends. 'And the first thing to say is that we have to give as much attention to the matter as we would in choosing a horse or armour. Is the person we aspire to befriend someone who is loving to those close to him? How does he treat his parents and siblings, his relatives? What is known of how he has dealt with both pleasure and difficulties in life?[39]

'Does he love money, does he get jealous? Is he a lover of fame, and addicted to being first? For if he is not generous, if he is intolerant of the equality that is essential to friendship, is he rivalrous, easily irritated and inclined to anger? Such a person is no candidate for friendship. Nor is he if he is over-much given to gambling or some other obsession.[40]

'Do not be friends with someone who has too many friends. It is not possible for large numbers to share sympathies, interests and tastes in the way that friendship requires. When some of his friends are delighted by the things that trouble others, which group will he favour? If one of his friends wishes him to share his pain, and another wishes him to go feasting with him, to which of the two will he go?'[41]

As the example of Diomedes and Sthenelus shows, it is good if the friends have opposite tendencies in being quick or slow to anger, energetic or languid in affairs. If these traits are complementary, the friends will match each other well, and be able to counterbalance and help each other. 'Such were the friendships of the past that won glorious remembrance,' Themistius says.[42]

As to keeping a friendship once gained: here too we must pay as much if not more attention as we would in keeping our weapons and tools in good order, or our garden. Friendship needs tending, and care. And when we have made the commitment to be someone's friend, we must honour it; that is what friendship is.

Put aside delay on every front. Share your friend's sufferings, be with him during his sleepless nights. Join with him when he is in danger, incurs expenses, and suffers disgrace. Do not wait to be invited to join with him. Rush to do it on your own. Keep anticipating what a given situation means. Try, in response to each need your friend has, to keep changing the role you play: play the part of physician when he is ill, of a lawyer when he is involved in a lawsuit, of an adviser on all occasions, of a helper when he has come to a decision . . . If fortune advances you, be sure to take your friend along with you.[43]

And for our purposes, finally, he urges that friends 'put aside rivalry, contentiousness and competitiveness, for friendship is not found among those who struggle against one another, but among those who aid one another in struggle'.[44]

The happiest chance that could befall a friendship, if for some reason it is not allowed a long and peaceful continuance, is to be sung by a poet. That is the case of the friendship between Nisus and Euryalus, Trojans in Aeneas' band in Italy, who died together in the course of a courageous military attempt. Theirs is a perennial in the list of classic friendships, and although it seems to acknowledge a homoerotic element much more clearly than in the case of the foregoing male pairs, Virgil is at some pains to avoid the implication.[45]

A Trojan band was being held at bay by a Rutulian force, cut off by it from their leader Aeneas. Two of the Trojans on guard that night were Nisus, a courageous warrior skilled in the use of javelin and spear, and Euryalus, 'than whom none was more beautiful among the Aeneadae . . . a boy, whose unshaven face showed the first bloom of youth'. They loved each other – 'one love was theirs' – and always fought side by side in battle.[46] As they kept watch Nisus was revolving a plan in his mind, to steal through the sleeping Rutulian camp so that he could get to Aeneas and tell him of their plight. He told it to Euryalus, who immediately insisted on going with him. Nisus tried to dissuade him, saying first that he wanted someone to perform his obsequies if he did not make it, and secondly that he did not want to risk depriving Euryalus' mother of her son. But Euryalus would not agree to be left out. So the two went to the leaders of the group to get their permission, which was willingly given.

As they made their way through the sleeping Rutulians, silently killing those in their path – Virigil describes the attendant gore with relish – Euryalus made the fatal mistake of being attracted by some of the armour available as plunder, including a glittering helmet. Just as the two were about to slip away into the safety of the woods beyond the Rutulian camp, a cavalry patrol was alerted to their presence by the gleam of Euryalus' stolen helmet, which he was now wearing.

Nisus had got safely away, but Euryalus, trailing behind weighed down with his plunder, was caught; and Nisus in a desperation of anxiety rushed back to help him. He saw that the Rutulians were about to kill Eurylaus in revenge for their dead comrades in the camp: 'truly maddened with fear, Nisus shouted aloud, unable to hide himself in the dark any longer, or endure such agony: "On me, Rutulians, turn your steel on me, me who did the deed! The guilt is all mine, he neither dared nor had the power; the sky and the all-knowing stars be witnesses: he only loved his unfortunate friend too much!"' But it was too late, The powerfully thrust blade of a sword drove through Euryalus' white breast, and he 'rolled over in death, and the blood flowed down his lovely limbs, and his neck, drooping, sank on his shoulder, like a bright flower scythed by the plough, bowing as it dies, or a poppy weighed down by a chance shower, bending its weary head'.[47]

All thought of getting to Aeneas forgotten in his grief, Nisus rushed among the Rutulians who had killed Euryalus, and revenged himself on as many as he could before their spears and swords overpowered him. 'Then, pierced through, he threw himself on the lifeless body of his friend, and found peace at last in the calm of death. Happy pair! If my poetry has the power, while the House of Aeneas lives beside the Capitol's immobile stone, and a Roman leader rules the Empire, no day will raze you from time's memory.'[48]

Virgil's promise has been kept. He first introduced the pair in the fifth book of the *Aeneid*, where they compete in the funeral games instituted by Aeneas for his father Anchises. Virgil enumerates those who gathered to take part, 'Nisus and Euryalus the foremost among them, Euryalus famed for his beauty, and in the flower of youth, Nisus famed for his devoted affection for the lad.'[49] What happens to them in their running race is both prophetic and illustrative. Nisus would have won if he had not slipped in some blood from a sacrificed bull. Had Nisus not slipped, Euralyus would have come third. But Nisus quick-wittedly uses his fall to trip the runner coming second, enabling Euryalus to win. In the end all three are given prizes.

Virgil calls the love between Nisus and Euryalus an *amor plus*. The intention is to make it seem to be a non-sexual devoted friendship, no doubt in deference to the Roman tradition that homosexuality in the army was severely frowned on. Homoeroticism anyway was not regarded as manly, even though it was tolerated; those who took the passive role in penetrative encounters were viewed with disfavour.

Nisus and Euryalus are cited among other reasons because they are a paradigm of a pair whose members are fully prepared to die for each other, 'greater love hath no man' being the theme. In the statue of them by Jean-Baptiste Roman in the Louvre, Nisus is shown protectively kneeling above the dying Euryalus, holding his hand, even as he looks up at the enemies who are killing him. One reading of the relationship has it that whereas in the Greek outlook a friendship between a pair such as Nisus and Euryalus might develop into a love affair, in Virgil – given the dignity and high tone of the *Aeneid*, consistent with the serious matter of the origins of Rome itself – such bonds move in the opposite direction, as with Plato; going beyond the carnal to something more like the spiritual, or at least the ethical.

Amys and Amylion in medieval romance, Enjolras and Grantaire in Hugo's *Les Misérables*, Annibal and Lerac in Dumas' *La Reine Margot*, and many others, are likened to the mythical princes Orestes and Pylades, who figure in every list of pairs of heroic friends; and their friendship is sung in Gluck's *Iphigénie en Tauride* and Handel's pasticcio *L'Oreste*.

Orestes is he who killed his mother in revenge for her murder of her husband, his father. The father was Agamemnon, the mother Clytemnestra, and the story of the House of Atreus' terrible fate was often told, not least by Aeschylus in the *Oresteia* trilogy, as well as in Sophocles' *Orestes*, and Euripides'

Iphigenia in Tauris. It is one of the great soap operas of world literature: Agamemnon had to sacrifice his daughter Iphigenia so that the Greek fleet could sail for Troy; in his ten-year absence a resentful Clytemnestra took a lover and with him plotted Agamemnon's death; in fulfilling his duty to avenge his father's murder, Orestes committed matricide and had to flee the torments of the Erinyes (the Furies), demon-deities whose job it is to punish those who kill their parents. He was finally freed from this agony by Athena and Apollo, who had him tried by the first ever sitting of the Court of the Areopagus in Athens, summoned on purpose for this trial; which acquitted him.

But the point of interest for lovers of friendships is that while Agamemnon was at Troy, Clytemnestra and her lover sent Orestes to live at the court of her relative King Strophus of Phocis. There he and his cousin Pylades were brought up together, and they formed a powerful and indissoluble friendship. When Orestes learned of his father's murder, he was encouraged in his plan of revenge by Pylades. In the adventures that followed, Pylades accompanied him everywhere. On one occasion they attempted to steal a statue of Artemis from Tauris but were caught and condemned to death; Orestes was struck mad by the Furies and Pylades nursed him back to sanity, wiping the foam from his mouth and tending him lovingly. The priestess of Artemis ordained that one of them had to die, the other had to take a message back to Greece. Orestes was chosen to be the messenger, Pylades to die, but Orestes refused, begging that Pylades be allowed to carry the message and that he be allowed to die in his place. The priestess turned out to be none other than Iphigenia, who had survived being sacrificed by her father, and she now recognised Orestes, whereupon the three made their escape together (taking the statue of Artemis with them).

The Greek writer of the second century CE who speaks of them as lovers more than friends is Lucian (if attribution to him of the *Erotes*, in Latin *Amores*, is correct).[50] In this dialogue the following account of them is given:

> 'Taking with them the god of love as the mediator of their mutual feelings, they sailed together on the same vessel of life ... as soon as they reached Tauris the Fury of mother-murderers was there and in the midst of the Taurides struck Orestes to the ground with madness. Pylades wiped away the foam and tended his frame, and sheltered him with a fine well-woven robe, in this way showing the feelings not only of a lover but of a father. When it was decreed that one was to go with a letter to Mycenae and the other to remain and be killed, each wished to be the one to remain so as to save the other, saying that he would live on in the continued life of his friend. And Orestes showed himself almost to be the lover rather than the beloved, in insisting that Pylades was the fitter to be the one to carry the letter.'[51]

Devotion, absolute loyalty, a passionate readiness to die in the other's place in order to save him: this combination is the key trope in these passionate friendships, and even if the occurrence of the trope in later literature was strictly homosocial, appeal to the example of Orestes and Pylades is always intended to evoke the bond's unyielding strength.

The medieval Orestes and Pylades, as noted, were Amys and Amylion, whose story gripped that period's imagination so strongly that it was told and retold, embellished and developed, in almost all the European traditions and languages including French, Latin, Norse, Welsh, German and Flemish. In the English version Amys and Amylion are brought up together, their passionate friendship forming in their early years before they are knighted in young adulthood. Various adventures result in Amylion contracting leprosy in punishment for a deception he engaged in to save his friend Amys. The two are told in simultaneous dreams that he can only be cured if he bathes in the blood of Amys' children. Amys kills his children and douses Amylion in their blood: he is cured, and the children are miraculously restored to life when this happens. Thereafter the two live together for the rest of their lives, and are buried together.

In the development of different versions a considerable backstory is invented. Amys is ordered to fight a duel, which Amylion successfully does on his behalf; later, when Amylion has wandered for three years in his diseased state, destitute and suffering, the two recognise each other because they each have one of a pair of matching gold cups. The devices of the plot, such as this, are predictable ones, the theme of loyalty and devotion is standard, but was so deeply attractive to its hearers and readers that the story became a classic.

'That *Amys and Amylion* was one of the most famous stories of friendship in the Middle Ages may seem surprising now,' writes Stephen Guy-Bray, 'as the poet relates what is, in effect, the story of a same-sex marriage and in doing so firmly subordinates both marriage and reproduction to homosocial concerns.'[52] This is true in the medieval versions; Victorian commentary more primly says that the two 'give up the remainder of their lives to the cause of charity'.[53] Spenser uses the story, but inversely, so to speak; Guy-Bray's study claims that he uses its tropes to support conventional romance and marriage. In Spenser's *The Squire of Low Degree* Aemylia is enclosed in a dungeon with a lustful monster, but her virginity is kept intact because every time the monster 'burnt in lustful fire' an old woman imprisoned with her 'instead supplied his bestiall desire'.[54] This is not laying down your life for your friend, but, so to speak, laying down for your friend. The theme of substitution in this case does not involve the love that the old woman ('hag', as Spenser calls her) and Aemylia bear each other, or a history of togetherness, so it is not a contribution to the literature of friendship, only of expediency. For it to be so, Aemylia would have to think of the 'hag' – and vice versa – as Montaigne thought of de La Boétie: 'each one gives himself so wholly to his friend . . . he is sorry that he is not double, triple, or quadruple, and that he has not several souls and several wills, to confer them all on this one object'. This adds reciprocity or mutuality to devotion, absolute loyalty, and a passionate readiness to die in the other's place.

These few examples of tales of friendship are the tip of an iceberg, whether in history, legend or story. Take a random sampling of each: in history Petronius and Nero, Hereward the Wake and Martin Lightfoot, Edward II and Piers Gaveston, Adams and Jefferson; in myth, to those already mentioned add Theseus and Pirithous, Damon and Pythias, Jason and his Argonauts, Arthur and Lancelot, Jane Frances de Chantal and

Francis de Sales; in story – where to start and stop? – Don Quixote and Sancho Panza, the Three Musketeers, Tom Sawyer and Huckleberry Finn, Chingachgook and Natty Bumppo, Miles Standish and John Alden, Jack Aubrey and Stephen Maturin, Tiberge and Des Grieux, Biddy and Pip, Holmes and Watson, Ratty and Mole, Biggles, Ginger and Bertie, Fred Flintstone and Barney Rubble, Harry, Ronald and Hermione – all three lists can be expanded to the scale of a dictionary, and not just because we do not quite know where the lines would be drawn to stop us. Are Fanny Price and Edmund Bertram friends? Are Cathy and Heathcliff friends? Do lovers and spouses whether fictional or otherwise fit into these lists, given that spouses can be enemies and at least some categories of lovers (O and René, for example) are scarcely friends?

Were the friends in these couples or groups to read the Hindu text known as *The Book of Good Counsels* they would be in agreement with it: 'That friend is the only true friend who is near when trouble comes . . . words are wind; deeds prove promise; he who helps at need is kin'; and again, 'He who shares his comrade's portion, be he beggar, be he lord/Comes as truly, comes as duly, to the battle as the board/He is friend, he is kinsman; less would make the name a lie.'[55]

It is plain common sense to accept that some of the great male friendships of myth, legend and history were doubtless homosexual loves. This raises interesting questions in thinking about friendship. To employ the crudest of generalisations and stereotypes for a moment: are male friendships which are homosexual loves like ordinary male friendships with sex involved, or are they like female friendships between men? That is, are they companionate relationships which are more about doing things together (as the stereotype depicts male friendships: going to football matches, helping each other fix the car) than communicating (as the stereotype depicts women's friendships: chatting at length about relationships, medical problems, gossip, the children)? Has the belated and welcome acceptance of homosexuality in society allowed one aspect of homosexual experience – the camp aspect: by a long chalk not all gays are camp – to become more salient as a parody of heterosexual relationships?

This is a complication in understanding what doubtless often is, and in the classical past almost certainly was meant to be, a *masculine* relationship – whether or not a homosexual one – in the sense that it did not ape heterosexual relationships and their associated role behaviours. (In any case these, in equally welcome ways, are now challenged as part of the process by which women liberate themselves from imprisoning stereotypes imposed by patriarchy.) Some homosexual stereotypes are deliberately and ironically camp, and there is a carry-over to relationships where one partner is regarded as the 'wife' (in the television sitcom *Modern Family* this is something of a running joke about the relationship between Cam and Mitchell, although the former – played by a straight actor – is clearly the 'wife' and the latter – played by a gay actor – is clearly the 'husband'). In the idealised version of classical homosexuality the roles of lover and beloved are defined by age and station; the lover is a man, the beloved a boy; the acceptable form of sexual congress (intercrural sex, or frottage of the man's penis between the boy's thighs[56]) tacitly respects the convention of not turning the boy into a female by playing the passive role in full penetration. It was, as noted, a scandal for some ancient commentators that Achilles, the younger, a practically beard-less youth, was thought by some to be the lover while Patroclus, the elder, was the beloved, for this inverted the proper order of things.

The point of raising these questions is that the idealised male friendships depicted in myth and legend are hard to understand if they are not in some sense fully masculine – they portray comrades in war together, adventuring together, with wives and families – while yet being loves in the fullest and most passionate sense, even though not all of them are acknowl-edged as sexual passions too. What was that relationship like? Does it belong to a seventh category, different from hetero-sexual male friendships, male–female non-sexual friendships, heterosexual female–female non-sexual relationships, contem-porary male homosexual relationships that mimic heterosexual relationships in partner balance, lesbian relationships, and standard male–female sexual relationships including marriage? And yet: these six categories are themselves very far from inter-nally homogeneous, and they neglect such further boundary-blurring phenomena as bisexuality and gender change. (Into which pigeonhole would one put the friendships between people one or more of whom used to be of a different sex?)

The more one itemises the permutations, the more one sees that it is plain silly to think that there are types of friendship that follow the contours of this stereotype or that. At the same time, it goes mightily against intuition to say so, because we are so wedded to our classifications: witness how readily people accept the caricatures of male and female friendships given above: men have companionate relationships involving activities (going to football matches, helping each other fix the car), while women have communicative relationships (talking about relationships, medical problems, the children – as if, in most societies, the women are not 'doing' far more than the men: in my childhood in Africa it was commonplace to see women – with babies strapped to their backs – pounding corn, carrying water, washing clothes in a river, hoeing a maize patch, while the men sat under a tree flapping idly at flies and chatting).

It is considerably easier to anatomise friendship into a set of identifiable patterns in history, when roles were imposed on people in vastly more rigid ways. The penalties for stepping outside a social and functional slot were great, and very few were in a position to do so, not least because their upbringing was directed at making it impossible to contemplate, even perhaps to imagine, alternatives. Consider a relatively late example: the position of young women in late eighteenth- and early nineteenth-century England, as depicted with such minuteness in Jane Austen's novels. The constraints they endured, the limited expectations they were allowed, seem to us suffocating now, and were doubtless experienced as such then; but there was no way out that was not highly fraught. But it makes it easy to say what external shape relations between people were meant – more accurately, permitted – to have. Today it is impossible to attempt classifications of types of friendship by gender, age, or any other of the lines of demarcation that we now see to be far too crude to be helpful – even, in fact, to be unhelpful.

But still the thought presses: were those legendary friendships, even when idealised, actually closer to a human norm that some powerful religious and social traditions had reason to oppose? It is sometimes said that the hostility to homosexuality in the Judaeo-Christian-Muslim tradition stems from the experience of the early Jewish people as herders of sheep and goats. Their very lives depended on the successful breeding of their flocks, so misdirection of sperm was a danger. One notes that in Old Testament morality it does not matter how many women a man sleeps with or has children by, or whether they are his wives, concubines or slaves; monogamy and its ills are a later gift of the deity. But woe to anyone who directs his seed other than to the womb of a woman. Onan was struck dead for spilling his on the ground in refusing to raise children to his dead brother's name;[57] which is therefore as bad as 'if a man lies with a man as one lies with a woman, both of them have committed an abomination; they shall surely be put to death; their blood is upon them'.[58] On this logic, masturbation is a worse crime than rape because at least the latter can result in pregnancy, which is all that matters.

The suppression of the classical outlook in Europe by an oriental one – in the form of Christianity – meant that male friendship had to assume a form, at least outwardly, in which it was never sexual in expression. As with anything pushed into hiding, it was more likely to accumulate aberrant margins. It is tempting to surmise how that affected the nature of the roles played; in a society where male homosexuality was accepted and even encouraged, a man need not cease to be one because he accepted or enjoyed the passive role in penetrative sex. In a setting where this role is by exclusive definition a female one, a man who accepts or enjoys playing it has opened himself to redefinition as – given the subordination of women and the throwing in of his sexual lot with them – 'less' than a man. And in the eyes of 'real' men, to lose status as male invites contempt, hatred, and even (given commonplace male anxieties about sexuality and potency) fear. Yet look at the social setting where this is not the reflex view: it is hard to see Euryalus or Patroclus or any other *eromenos* of legend as less than a 'real man' in whatever macho way, exclusive of sexual behaviour, you care to mention.

All these examples of friendship can be understood as iterating the simple thought that friendship embodies not just camaraderie and enjoyment, which any acquaintances might share, but a deeper tie with an essentially mutual character, however that works in practice; it is at least supportive, forgiving, and durable, when it is at its best.

Durability has two meanings: robustness under pressure, and survival over a long period. In friendship it is desirable in both senses, and old friendships might by that very fact be the best kind; but the 'long period of time' sense is not necessary. Friendships do not fail to count as such because they end; it is common enough for people who were friends in the fullest and richest sense to cease to be so after a time, for any number of reasons, even if they are usually bad ones.

This was the case with Samuel Taylor Coleridge and William Wordsworth, whose dozen years of intimacy changed English poetry, and who fell out at last because of misunderstandings and hurt feelings rather than any shift in their philosophies. While their friendship lasted they understood each other's genius, and felt the highest mutual respect, as well as real affection. Even when Coleridge's gifts were obviously running into the sands of opium and alcohol, Wordsworth and his family continued to house him and encourage him, and Wordsworth himself continued to hope for Coleridge's help in the grand project they had together envisioned: the writing of a monumental philosophical poem.

But Coleridge was an undisciplined addict who preferred to talk than write, which is harder work by far; and who left too little of his genius behind him – a few brilliant poems and poetic fragments, along with sometimes suggestive, sometimes insightful, but too often disorganised lucubration.

Meanwhile Wordsworth was an increasingly prickly and self-important lone male in a household of admiring women (with consequences Coleridge had foreseen and warned against), so between the two poets a falling-out was inevitable. There later rose from its ashes a thin and faltering acquaintanceship, from which no flame of their earliest comradeship ever again flickered.[59]

Equally productive during the time it lasted was the already mentioned brilliant friendship (for this it was, even more than a love affair) between Voltaire and the remarkable Emilie, marquise du Châtelet, one of the most unfairly neglected (because a woman, and an aristocratic one at that) contributors to the growth of modern science. She translated Newton into French at her home, the Château de Cirey, and her theoretical work on the nature of light is seminal.

The relationship of these two brilliant souls was full of fun and storms, the balance between the two shifting from a preponderance of the former to the latter as time passed. It was an erotic comradeship in its first years, and just a comradeship in its later years; and it was political, not least in the sense that Emilie protected Voltaire as best she could from the injudiciousness of some of his writings. But above all it was an intellectual friendship, in which each encouraged the other, directly and by example, to produce some of their best work.

It was not without escapades, as when Voltaire had to flee arrest in the middle of the night, or when Emilie paid their debts by fiddling the lottery and dreaming up tax-farming schemes. There is always much to enjoy in the record of sharp wits and high achievement, especially in uncertain times of the kind those two free spirits inhabited.[60]

People most often write about their friends when they have died, when they have the freedom to say more than they might in non-obituary mode. In these writings may be found the minutiae which lie far below the surface generalities that a treatise of friendship has to deal in. They are the proof that friendships might have large structural similarities, sometimes surprisingly so given other differences that obtain; but that each is still individual and possibly eccentric.

One has to turn to such accounts to see why and how. There is a variously striking, moving and delicious collection of such called *The Company They Kept*, put together by Robert Silvers and Barbara Epstein. Each piece is an obituary reminiscence of an outstanding individual: Stanley Kunitz on Theodore Roethke, Robert Lowell on Randall Jarrell, Derek Walcott on Robert Lowell, Edward Dahlberg on Hart Crane, Robert Oppenheimer on Albert Einstein, Anna Akhmatova on Modigliani, Saul Bellow on John Cheever, Joseph Brodsky on Isaiah Berlin, Tatyana Tolstaya on Joseph Brodsky, Seamus Heaney on Thomas Flanagan – it is a formidable catalogue. Their variety throws more light on the diversity and possibilities of friendship than a treatise like this one can.

One way they do so is by their generosity. As obituary reminiscences (not obituaries as such) they might predictably be generous: we are mostly wedded to the principle *de mortuis nil nisi bonum* after all – 'of the dead say nothing but good' – even if its pieties too often require us to be hypocritical for a time, and form a barrier to expression of franker, more honest feelings we might have for the deceased. But the sense in these accounts is not of forced generosity, but of real liking and respect. Prudence Crowther says of S. J. Perelman: 'Perelman was one of those people who make you feel as charming as they are.' Derek Walcott told Robert Lowell that he liked the tie he was wearing: 'He took it off and gave it to me.' Jason Epstein recalls Edmund Wilson's refusal in old age to accept a hearing aid, a pacemaker, vaccinations, or Thomas Mann's metaphysics. Saul Bellow picks out exactly the right quotation from John Cheever to illustrate the latter's purpose: 'The constants that I look for,' Cheever wrote, 'are a love of light and a determination to trace some moral chain of being.' Enrique Krauze does the same for Octavio Paz, who described women as 'the gate of reconciliation with the world'.

Some people have a knack for being loved by the world at large, and Albert Einstein was one of those. The revolution he wrought in physics is a giant fact of history, but less well known is the failure of his final quarter-century. Robert Oppenheimer acutely remarks, 'He had a right to that failure.' His disappointment largely arose from his inability – despite persistent efforts – to show that quantum theory, which he had fathered but deeply disliked, was internally inconsistent.

Darryl Pinckney, in an essay as much about his own first unsuccessful attempt at life in New York as about his ostensible subject, Djuna Barnes, brings the latter into vivid focus in her old age, in one small cluttered room, struggling with mortality but still bright-eyed, like a tiny bird that will not give up the desire to fly.

Not all the friendships related here would be called such by observers: Susan Sontag never felt that she liked Paul Goodman much, but missed him when he died, and Robert Craft's relationship with Igor Stravinsky is one that goes as far beyond friendship as it fails to approach its normal lineaments. But all this does is to show how variously and strangely people's lives become intertwined, so that when the relationship ends – in these cases because of death, that absurd and imponderable interruption of so much creativity and intelligence – there is at very least regret, and a large preparedness to understand.[61]

There should be more such books. For as one says: one could go on. There is the Bloomsbury Group, the friendships among the members of which were creative, not least in giving scope for what has been called 'the higher bitchery' too. They – an extended list would include Virginia Woolf and her sister Vanessa Bell, Clive Bell, Roger Fry, Lytton Strachey, at a pinch John Maynard Keynes, and other lesser lights – were inspired by G. E. Moore's view in *Principia Ethica* that the highest values, the ones chiefly worth pursuing and realising in life, are beauty and friendship; so they economised by having beautiful friends. Before and after them other groups of friends likewise made coteries of creativity – the Shelleys and Byron in Italy, Picasso, Braque and Apollinaire in Paris at the beginning of the twentieth century, Robert Graves, Siegfried Sassoon and Wilfred Owen recuperating at Craiglockhart in 1917, the Algonquin round table in New York, the Toynbee–Nicolson lunch club in

1950s' London: one could accumulate many instances. Not every member of such groups produced work of lasting value, but if one or some did it was in part because of the materials provided and the encouragement given by being among friends. In such cases friends are the *interlocuteurs valables* who provide the safe ground for trying things out, the first audience and critics, the refuge from failure.

Coleridge and Wordsworth provide examples of two people of high talent fostering each other's early abilities. Another example is the pairing of T. S. Eliot and Ezra Pound, without whom there would not be *The Waste Land* we have. Less well known is the fact that George Eliot only wrote fiction in the twenty years she and G. H. Lewes lived together. Lewes was a philosopher and biographer of real talent – his Life of Goethe has yet to be bettered, and his *Biographical History of Philosophy* was an inspiration to the present writer at school. Eliot read to him every evening what she had written in the day; he was her sounding-board. When he died she ceased to write fiction, no longer having the safe ear of such a friend.

Were Dr Johnson and Boswell friends? They were very unequal in character, age and outlook, but there is something Godwinian in the need that Johnson seemed to have for his otherwise irritating and inquisitive little companion, who devoted his time to whoring and – only a little differently by choice of organ – poking his nose into other people's business. He went, for example, to snuffle around Hume as the latter lay on his deathbed, to see how an atheist faces extinction. But he might have played a friend's role to Johnson in life as he has certainly played one for Johnson's reputation ever since. Friends tell each other about their lives, feelings, anxieties and hopes; in this respect they do the service of the confessional; to talk to a biographer might well feel like that. And so friendship would enter, if by another window.

What more lyrical lament is there for a lost friend than Tennyson's *In Memoriam A. H. H.*[62] The friend was Arthur Henry Hallam, whom Tennyson met when they were undergraduates together at Trinity College, Cambridge. Hallam was a poet himself, and a friend of Gladstone, with whom he had been at Eton. When he and Tennyson met they fell instantly and deeply into friendship, like Jonathan and David. The tie between them was strengthened when Hallam fell in love with Tennyson's sister Emily, and the two planned to become engaged. The death of his father meant that Tennyson had to leave Cambridge, and he also needed Hallam's help with the publication of his first two volumes of poetry. Their plans to publish a joint volume of poetry never had a chance to materialise. Hallam was a mere twenty-two when he died suddenly of a cerebral stroke while in Vienna, travelling with his father.

Tennyson writes of walking in the street where Arthur had lived, to the door 'where my heart was used to beat/So quickly, waiting for a hand'; all the light has gone out of the places they used to meet, 'For all is dark where thou art not.' He thinks of the ship bearing Arthur's body home, and asks the winds to sleep 'as he sleeps now,/My friend, the brother of my love,/My Arthur, whom I shall not see/Till all my widow'd race be run;/Dear as the mother to the son,/More than my brothers are to me.' He thinks of himself as a widower, and feels 'A void where heart on heart reposed;/And, where warm hands have prest and closed.' He and 'The human-hearted man I loved' walked the track of life 'with equal feet'; pain was halved because it was shared with him. The word Tennyson consistently uses to describe their mutual feeling is 'love'.

Moreover it is love – 'the spirit of true love' – that reassures him when he anxiously wonders whether the soul of his lost friend will detect him in sin, seeing him think or do something dishonourable: 'Thou canst not move me from thy side,/Nor human frailty do me wrong . . . So fret not, like an idle girl,/that life is dashed with flecks of sin.' The admonition not to behave like a girl prompts a simile: 'My spirit loved and loves him yet/ Like some poor girl whose heart is set/On one whose rank exceeds her own.'

The metaphor of widowhood is Tennyson's choice for explaining his loss. 'Two partners of a married life— /I look'd on these and thought of thee/In vastness and in mystery,/And of my spirit as of a wife.' In revisiting Cambridge, and thinking of their time together, Tennyson acknowledges himself as the Patroclus, the Pylades of the pair, though not in those words; he remembers Arthur's effect on others, 'While I, thy nearest, sat apart,/And felt thy triumph was as mine . . . Nor mine the sweetness or the skill,/But mine the love that will not tire, And, born of love, the vague desire/That spurs an imitative will.'

The poem's correlative religious themes – for it is a religious poem too; although of religious doubt in the face of science, and of a substitution of love itself as the agent of salvation – do not do much to assuage the intense grief it expresses. The hope of being posthumously reunited with those lost to death is said to sustain many grievers who have a religious faith, but there is little of that here. Rather the loss of one so loved seems to be inconsolable. But in a later canto Tennyson speaks to a new friend, saying that he cannot transfer the whole of the love he felt for his first friend, for it was 'First love, first friendship, equal powers,/That marry with the virgin heart'. All the same, he cannot remain friendless for ever; 'My heart, tho widow'd, may not rest/Quite in the love of what is gone,/but seeks to beat in time with one/That warms another living breast.'

The evidence of the poem itself would prompt questions about whether the deep sentiment it displays is homosocial or homosexual, and the answer would probably be the latter. But the biographical evidence is against the textual evidence; Hallam loved Tennyson's sister, and in the poem there is mention of the lost opportunity for Tennyson to dandle Hallam's sons on his knee. The fact that Tennyson married and had children (the eldest called Hallam) is irrelevant, because many homosexual and bisexual men marry and have children. More to the point is to ask whether sentimental expressions of affection without literal implications of homosexuality were not after all more acceptable in the period; there was no outcry by Tennyson's readers of the kind that other Victorians, not very much later, raised against Oscar Wilde.

From the point of view of understanding Tennyson's take on friendship, we see that it is greatly more encompassing than the conventional part of what he says – 'O friendship, equal-poised control,/O heart, with kindliest motion warm' – for the avowals of love and the feminine posture of grief permit a much more extreme sense of loss, consonant with a much more loving and strongly bonded relationship. Some might say that this friendship, like the foregoing legendary ones, was a friendship of youth; had Hallam survived and married Emily and made a success at law (even Tennyson said he would not have been a good poet) it is possible that they would have ended as the Victorians liked to say Amys and Amylion did: by devoting their lives to charitable causes.

And there is a point here. We expect the friendships of youth to be intense, those of middle and old age to be mellow, even if they are not long-standing ones. Is this true? Not invariably so, but often and perhaps most often so. It would follow just from the respectively more and less impetuous, urgent, striving nature of youth and age; it would reflect the insight behind the remark 'When young I loved Ovid, now that I am old I love Horace.' There is a difference here with erotic love: it can be felt with as much intensity in the middle and later years as in youth, if the right spark is put to the right tinder. When passion is ignited between older people of similar age it does not occasion comment, but it is disapproved of between partners considerably different in age. Few can believe, in such cases, that any of the reasons people might have for falling in love apply as fully here as elsewhere; even that the motive is a mature conception of the finest possibilities implicit in the circumstance. That is perhaps a lack of imagination; the conventions currently in play tell us that it is not.

PART III

Experiences

CHAPTER 8

Friendship Viewed

Consider these two claims: first, that friendship is one of the two most significant kinds of relationship that human individuals can have with each other – the other being intimate love, itself a various and multiple phenomenon – and secondly, that there are no rules setting out the rights and responsibilities of friendship. Between them these claims alert us to the complex nature of the relationship which is, second only to the bond of intimacy between lovers in the honeymoon of their love, the most important contributor to the possibility of good human lives. To say this is not to undervalue the other great contributors – creativity, knowledge and discovery, pleasure – but there is every reason to think that these are in any case connected in more and less direct ways with friendships, in ways suggested later.

For this reason the major intellectual traditions of the world, both Eastern and Western, are rich in discussions of friendship, and Part I was a survey of some in the Western tradition. There are many kinds of friendship, achieved by many different routes, and although they have a set of central features in common – at least in their idealised versions – which include affection, sympathy and loyalty, their additional dimensions are determined partly by time, place and culture, and partly by the individuality of those between whom they arise.

It is an interesting coincidence, and perhaps more, that Mencius in ancient China thought the same as Aristotle in ancient Greece: that a friend is 'another self'. If one cares about someone else in the best way of friendship, both of these thinkers claimed, his good matters as much to oneself as one's own, making a pair of friends 'one mind in two bodies'. As noted several times above, most will justifiably think that this overstates the case, even in those rare iconic instances celebrated in literature – David and Jonathan, Nisus and Euryalus – which as we have seen could be examples of love more romantic than companionate. It indicates the way that friendship has been taken to be more than just camaraderie and the sharing of experience and enjoyment, but a mutual tie which at its best, and during its best period, is supportive, forgiving and durable.

Why is this so? The answer lies in the psychological facts underlying human sociality. Human beings are essentially social animals, 'essentially' having the force of 'that which crucially defines'. Relationships are vital not just to the well-being but to the identity of all but the oddest individuals. Explicitly intimate relationships tend to be few in number (restricted as they are to family and lovers) and idiosyncratic in character, and they play a deep role in forming individuality. But it is also a person's range of more general friendships that helps to shape his or her social personae – note the plural – especially in the formative period of youth.

There are different ways of expressing the point about the formativeness of friendships, most familiarly perhaps by invoking the idea of peer influence, which in turn is most obvious in adolescence. But it is important not to restrict the idea of friendship to people who are alive at the same time, despite this being the main category. For one can have friendships with writers long dead, with characters in their books, with historical figures, even (after a fashion) with animals – typically pet dogs, cats and horses. One good way to know what sort of person someone is, is to examine the kinds of friendship he or she has maintained through time, including these non-standard ones.

The desideratum always of course remains: to know what we mean by 'friendship'. But the sheer variety and nuance of relationships which deserve the name, given their overlaps with other kinds of relationships and the infinite gradations on all sides into relationships that are more informatively described as something else, make this exceedingly hard. We might say that it requires an understanding at least of the central varieties; but this is only partly true, because there the temptation is to focus on clichés, however accurate and informative these might be.

If we succumb for a moment to the last-named route, we see that both received wisdom and the models offered us by the philosophical and literary debate, at least when they are sufficiently down to earth, jointly have it that a friend is a person one likes who returns one's affection and concern; who shares some of one's interests and attitudes; who gives when asked or even without being asked; who understands, or tries to, without being too judgemental; who is loyal and constant, rejoicing at good fortune and supporting through bad; who tells unpleasant truths and pleasant untruths when either is necessary; whose affection is freely given, not bartered for services or advancement or other interest; and who makes the innocent and proper assumption that all the claims, expectations, rights and duties of this vital and valuable human bond are reciprocal.

Reciprocity is indispensable. This of course is meant primarily in relation to living contemporaries, but indirectly it applies to friendships with the authors and characters of admired books, say; there is indeed a kind of reciprocity even here, for someone gets something – it might be very much – from a book, which (as we put it) 'repays' thoughtful and attentive reading.

The human–human case of reciprocity is however the one at issue here. Where one party to a relationship is the giver and the other the taker of regard, kindness, affection and support, the relationship might better be described differently, as a patron–client one (if it is between unrelated individuals) or as a kin relationship, typically cross-generational as with parent and child.

Indeed perhaps the most important human relationship is the parenting, and especially mothering, of small children, a very unequal affair although a certain reciprocity exists – the child loves, needs and depends upon the mother, which can give the mother a profound sense of self-worth and satisfaction. But even this relationship has friendship as part of its ultimate goal, if successful: if friends are independent partners in their relationship, achieving friendship with one's offspring means that the project of helping them grow into freedom has worked.

One cannot talk of friendship without inevitably coming up against the subject of love – love in its various guises, but love most especially of what (following the distinctions drawn by the ancient Greeks) are called *storge, pragma*, and *ludus*, where *storge* connotes the natural affection of kin ties, *pragma* the bond that grows out of companionship and shared interests, and *ludus* the lighter and less committed interchanges of playful camaraderie. In the view of some, it is only by stretching the notion of friendship somewhat that one would include in this list *agape*, the benevolent concern for one's fellow human beings in general. In the first three cases at least, we are as apt to talk of affection and warmth as of love, while distinguishing them from *eros* with its explicitly sexual connotation, and relatedly with what the Greeks named *mania* and which we now call romantic love or even (when we accord it less dignity) infatuation, because we wish to separate these latter from the forms of interpersonal bonds not exclusively premised on sexual attraction and desire.

But as we know, complications arise in friendship between the sexes if they involve sex and, as we have copiously seen, some male friendship has historically been presented as the outward form of homoerotic love. When sexual elements enter heterosexual friendship, socially constructed attitudes to sex disrupt the classification we are inclined to give the previous relationship, so that at very least we move it to a different place psychologically, to make it conform to the place it now occupies physiologically – even if the friendship remains and the sexual activity stops. In this connection a disappointed would-be lover does not appreciate hearing the words, 'I like you as a friend', precisely because they imply that the relationship desired by the utterer is at most in the *pragma–ludus* family of affections and not at all in the desired *eros–mania* one.

The question of friendship between individuals of opposite sex is an intriguing one. Can there be cross-sex friendships which are genuinely like non-sexual same-sex friendships? Sceptics are inclined to think that such a thing could exist only before and after the courting age, by which is meant the period between the respective onsets of puberty and (if we allow them to be this harsh) middle age. The facts would seem to be against the sceptics, given that most of us can cite obvious cases of individual men and women enjoying non-sexual friendships.

Perhaps the real question here concerns not whether such friendships are possible, but the degree to which they are like same-sex non-sexual friendships. Surely, some might say, the uncontroversial fact that there can be differences of perspective and experience between the sexes makes cross-sex friendships different from same-sex ones. It would hardly be surprising if this were true, and if it were so, such friendship would surely be all the more valuable for it. But it would be friendship still, and – to repeat – friendship takes many forms.

'Friendship takes many forms': in fact this truism represents both a problem and an opportunity. The wide variety of forms that interpersonal connections can take while meriting the name of friendship shows different characteristics and different degrees of strength according to circumstance. A person's sense of self is a composite of influences and reactions to influences, not least the influences of the people whom she admits into her confidence because she likes, trusts and is interested in them. Each individual is in truth a plurality and needs to express different sides of herself in different settings, which is one of the prime ways in which having a variety of friends is invaluable.

It has been well said that no single other person can meet all one's needs and interests, which reinforces this point. The problem this raises is that it frustrates any attempt to give a single neat definition of friendship. The opportunity it offers is that friendship can be explained by examples, so that by drawing from discussions of friendship and cases of it one can illustrate its various aspects, and see how they reveal through the veil of differences one of the supremest of the values that make life worth living. That is why we have to turn from the abstractions of the philosophers to the makers of myth and story, and the writers of history and its personal form, biography, to have a chance of seeing individual pebbles in the mosaic, so that when we step back to see the whole, even if we do not see it differently, we see it true.

CHAPTER 9

Friendship Examined

Because this is an examination of the *idea* of friendship offered by the tradition of debate and portrayal in our sources, and because we have seen the consensus agree with reason that friendship is a great good, indeed one of the highest available to us, we must now set that claim to work. But before doing so, we have to try to answer some questions.

We say that friendship is a great good, and both the philosophical and literary portrayals canvassed in earlier chapters give us lists of reasons why. Let us inspect them.

We think we know what the philosophers mean when they say that friendship is an intrinsic good – good in itself, not for any other reason than that it is good, thus excluding the good things that friendship brings us and does for us, for mention of them introduces the idea of instrumentality, from which high-mindedness recoils. This recoil can be justified in light of examples of dishonest, hypocritical or deceitful cases of 'false friendship', which has a particularly bad name in that it trades on the bond of trust constitutively implicit in friendship, in order to betray it for the advantage of the betrayer. But friendships can be of many kinds of mutual usefulness without being hypocritical or deceitful. Friendships can and often do grow from the mutual help and advantage that interpersonal relationships supply. In fact, in the practice of life it is hard to see how any friendship can be characterised as other than a trade-off, because it is typically a trade-off of a very good and pleasing kind, at very least giving pleasure, comfort and happiness to the parties when they are enacting their friendship together. It would seem that a purist (Kant, or Aristotle when he is thinking of the most elevated form in his hierarchy of friendships) would have to downplay what it is that friendship actually does for people

We should therefore be unabashed in answering the question, Why is friendship good and valuable? by listing the pleasure, the fun, the utility and the advantage that come from a strong mutual liking between people who are interested in each other's welfare and benefit, and who help each other because of that interest. All these things are goods too, whose possession enhances the quality of our experience of life. But there is of course more. We say that friends share things: not just the pleasure already mentioned, but knowledge and experience, and also burdens and difficulties. These latter prompt the thought that comfort, solace and sympathy are profoundly valuable gifts of friendship in times of trouble, which no one seeks a friend for – we do not think 'I must make some friends just in case, in future, I suffer grief or illness, and might need them' as the chief reason for having them; it is likely that we never consider this when making friends – but for which having a friend is an immense good.

When talk of 'sharing' waxes sentimental it principally means experience – the magazine version would probably focus on laughter and tears, holidays, secrets – but it does not often mean actual sharing of (say) one's income or one's wife. In antiquity sharing had this more demanding character, of sharing one's substance with friends, and even sharing their fate – going into exile with them, say. It is harder to do these things now that our social arrangements and conventions are so much more complex and pigeonholed. It is not a matter of just sharing your cloak with your friend when it rains or is cold on a military campaign. Duty to one's family raises a question mark over sharing your income with someone outside the family, even a very dear friend. These days to give a friend a helping hand in her career smacks not of friendship but of corruption. We still, happily, accept a friend's help with replastering the kitchen, digging up a flower bed, pushing the broken-down car off to the side of the road, making the cakes for the children's party, and the like.

One good thing about friendship which has survived changes in social conventions is that it is a resource of guidance and correction. A loyal friend whom one trusts can tell us when we are going wrong, reprove us, advise us, can suggest a course of action when we are wavering in a dilemma, can stand up for us or do something for us when we need an ally. She can also tell us helpful lies when we need reassurance or calming down.

If you think of someone who has no friends you see what can happen: a human being, like a neglected garden, may become rather overgrown – quite literally dirty and unkempt, unsocial, introverted; after a bit, eccentric or half mad. Social intercourse keeps people – quite literally – clean and reasonably polite, sane and functional; how much more so does having friends help to keep people functioning in ways that they often do not if left in the void of friendlessness.

Such are some of the goods of friendship. But friendship has its negative aspects and dangers too. One is that when we make friends, we contract for grief. This is the same for love. Inevitably, one of any pair (save for the rare cases of both being in the same plane crash) is going to be bereft of the other – by death, by divorce, by the drifting apart that time brings as people and circumstances change. In the latter case the drifting apart might be mutual, scarcely noticed, and no great sorrow to either. But death or a quarrel or a betrayal: these cause suffering, and do harm. A friend gets cancer, worsens through many trials of surgery and chemotherapy, and dies under one's eyes: this is a burden we willingly and actively accept out of love for her, but it is no less painful for the willingness.

The pangs of betrayal in friendship have their own special character. In too many cases betrayal or a bitter quarrel leads to hostility; friendship becomes enmity, friends become enemies – all made worse in cases where the erstwhile friends are still to some extent embrangled, with mutual friends, membership of the same tennis club, working together in the same company or school – such complications ramify.

Some friendships can be ruined by becoming sexual; some can be enhanced by it, whether as 'friendships with benefits' (the parties are rather inelegantly called 'fuck buddies' by some) or by turning into a romantic or spousal relationship. In the former case they provide an affirmative answer to the question whether friendships can be sexual as well as being friendships; examples of the latter are not necessarily part of a negative answer to the same question.

Some, among them certain Christian thinkers, think that friendship is not a good because it is preferential and exclusive. To have a friend is to put others lower down the scale of one's interest and concern for one's fellow humans. A disproportionate amount of one's resources, whether of time or substance, is devoted to friends, resources which could be shared more equitably with others. By putting a friend's interest above that of others, the latter could actually be disadvantaged, and unfairly so.

The dangers of friendship are of course the worst of the negative side, and one of them flows from the partiality just mentioned. It is not only that one might deal unjustly with others in light of one's partialities, but that one's judgement might be distorted, and one could even do serious wrongs in the name of friendship, giving bad advice and breaching moral imperatives or breaking the law in helping a friend to do bad things, or at least in fostering interests which are not worthy ones. That requires a judgement about which things are worthy and which unworthy, and that is where more general ethical reflection does its work, so that one now sees an additional motivation for it: that clarity in this respect has a chance of making one a better friend to one's friends.

So: a bad thing about friendship is what happens if one is a bad friend to one's friends. Another way to be a bad friend is to be injudicious in one's own actions in ways that harm one's friends. Arguably, Timon of Athens was a bad friend to those around him because he acted unreasonably, first by being over-lavish in his generosity, and then by lurching completely to the other extreme and being comprehensively misanthropic, even though it was only a few who had been examples to him of ingratitude, and of betrayal of the bond he thought he had established with them through his generosity.

In the temptations it offers to be too partial, too generous, too dismissive of the competing claims of others who might have some claim too, friendship risks being at odds with other things regarded as goods. The ancients taught moderation in all things – 'nothing too much' was one of the Delphic oracle's injunctions – and if that applies to friendship, then we should not love friends too much, give them too much of our time or substance, and the like. Is the idea of not being 'too much' of a friend consistent with the idea of the selflessness sometimes required of friendship, the unstinting aid when really needed, the wholeheartedness of the commitment? Aristotle's ethics of reason enjoined the 'middle way', identifying the virtues by their occupancy of a moral space between opposing vices – generosity between meanness and profligacy, courage between cowardice and rashness, and so on. Should the virtues of friendship be calibrated between the vices of hostility and – presumably – servile adoration? Well: perhaps so, in this case, because it is not clear that servile adoration would be in a friend's interests anyway. And perhaps 'calibrate' is not the right verb; 'judge' is better. We do well to judge when a friend needs help, advice, admonition, unconditional acceptance and affection, sympathy, being left alone, and so on.

So in this case the application of reason to the question of how far one needs to go in the different interests and circum-stances of friendship is appropriate. The real concern about the place of reason in friendship is a different pair of vices: a cold rationality that really does measure and weigh the degrees of commitment and activity that one is prepared to give friends, on the one hand, and on the other the irrationality induced by too great a partiality for friends. This is implicated in talk of bad outcomes above, but there is a more general point, which is that whereas there are non-rational good things (pleasant sensations are an example) there is never anything good about irrationality. If friendship overthrows one's judgement to the extent that one does irrational things, then friendship is harmful. And it often is so. The group of buddies go out for a drink; they have too many, and egg one another on to do silly things in the jollity that ensues; risky things perhaps – climbing up a high wall to teeter along it, running across a train track – with tragic consequences perhaps.

Another matter that merits further consideration is the 'another self' trope started by Aristotle – as mentioned in what was more or less an aside, but pounced on by many since. There is a metaphorical use of this which is unexceptionable. I rather think Montaigne's beautiful memorial to his friendship with Etienne de La Boétie treats the idea of the merging of two selves into one as an effort to emphasise unity of outlook and interest, of agreement, not of the loss of self in another's self, or the submerging of two identities into a corporate or joint identity. For this would be to deny much of what is good and important about friendship in the first place.

The quickest way to make this point is to remember that we value autonomy, self-determination, and the construction and enhancement of a personal identity, as very high goods in themselves. To honour these things in another is to be a friend to that other. To respect the autonomy of another, her right to the final say on important decisions and choices, is to be a good friend to her. To want to subsume that separateness, to deny or bridge it too closely, is to lose sight of the good of individuality. And in fact the idea of two or more individuals whose differences are complementary and interesting, who respect each other as different and whose differences are accepted, tolerated, admired or honoured, is the very stuff of mature friendship.

The idea of the separateness that allows for complementarity is not merely implicit, it is explicit in the idealised classical versions of antiquity. Take almost any example – Nisus and Euryalus, let us say, as described earlier. Both were young, but Euryalus was significantly younger. Nisus had a reputation – *acerrimus armis*, most swift in arms – as a tried and tested warrior. Euryalus, less tested than Nisus, was a beardless youth, beautiful, and devoted to his heroic older partner. They form a type of a pair of fitting complementarity. Now, they might love one another so deeply that they are willing to sacrifice their lives for one another; they are inseparable, venturing all things together; Nisus (as the foot race example shows) is prepared to do wrong in the interests of his friend, which a more austere theoretician of friendship would frown on. But they are not twins. One of the ideas that grew out of the 'another self' trope was the idea that twins are exemplars of what friends should be – identical twins, that is, who often (especially when young) do seem to be two halves of a single person.[1] But this goes fully against the idea that friendship is a relationship of respect between autonomous individuals whose mutuality is freely and willingly given, not taken automatically out of a common pool.

In fact the idea of 'another self' contradicts another of the desiderata attached to idealisations of friendship: that friends should be other-interested in their friendship, not self-interested.

But if friends are one single self, then anything done for the other's good is *ipso facto* done for one's own good. Other-interest is self-interest; it is not the friend but oneself for whom one acts. When an argument collapses into absurdity as this does, one sees that it is of course not what is intended; but it is the result of taking the 'another self' trope too seriously. The very idea of a bond, of sharing, of giving, of mutuality, is predicated on the idea of a duality or more: it seems essential to friendship that it should be a relationship between 'Others'.

CHAPTER 10

The Two Claims

At the beginning of Chapter 8 above it was said that a familiar pair of claims is made about friendship: first, that it 'is one of the two most significant kinds of relationship that human individuals can have with each other – the other being intimate love, itself a various and multiple phenomenon – and secondly, that there are no rules setting out the rights and responsibilities of friendship'.

Reflection on these claims suggests two surprising thoughts: that it is an ethical obligation actively to pursue friendship; and that friendship as the desired terminus of all relationships therefore trumps other relationships.

Consider the nature of the good and well lived life, the flourishing life which feels good to live because it involves endeavour, satisfying in itself, towards the realisation of worthwhile goals, and because it is, or in the main and sum is, positive in its impact on others to whom the agent owes responsibility – which in attenuating circles of concern might be the whole human race, indeed the planet. Now if friendship is one of the high goods in such a life, and if we agree with Aristotle – as I think we must – that without it the rest of the edifice of good in life would crash down, then it is a duty to ourselves and others that we are friends, that we have friends, that we promote friendship, that we reflect on it, choose it, look after and foster it. In just the same way as we reflect on and choose other valuable things to live by, so we must reflect on and choose friendships.

This involves us in thinking how to be a friend, as well as thinking about what we want from friendship, and therefore what we want in our friends. Here another point presses to be remembered. No one other person will ever satisfy all the interests, needs and desires that each individual typically has. People might if lucky be deeply and happily in requited love with a wonderful other, but still need friends and colleagues, acquaintances, and sustained relationships with family members. Most people can give love to and receive love from more than one other person, and most people need to. This suggests that more than one friendship is requisite, even if we have one particular friend who answers to that part of oneself that is most oneself, most central to one's naked identity, most acutely conscious of itself as desiring mutuality with another close to it.

It is possible to see family, acquaintances and workmates as answering to the less exigent aspect of one's need for community, leaving just one or a very few entrances for particular friends, 'real friends' as people say in marking the distinction, whom one admits to psychological places that the others cannot go.

The phrase 'real friend' suggests something else. There are friends who are genuinely so, in being much closer and more privileged than acquaintances are, but with whom the connection has features that place limits on it. The pieties of those who say that there is 'no true friendship' (the 'no true Scotsman' again) involved in mutual usefulness, or even in one-sided usefulness, are merely that: pieties. There is no reason why mutually useful or even unilaterally useful (though there is almost always a benefit of some kind to such transactions) friends cannot both be and think themselves so. We distinguish between friendship of any stripe and relationships in which hypocrisy, cheating and insincerity attend the motives for the connection, by means of those very words. If 'A and B are friends' is a true proposition, then by definition none of hypocrisy, cheating and insincerity is involved. Now, if such a relationship evolved into a 'real friendship' – a much closer one, where the utility aspect is no longer relevant to the fact of friendship even if it is still there – would it not have been a friendship before? It is temerity to legislate that a friendship can only be one if it begins in a pure, non-utilitarian, perfectly mutual and equal moment. Not all do; perhaps not many do.

Recall that 'ethics' and 'morals' have different meanings. Morality is part of ethics, but ethics is a larger and more inclusive notion. Ethics is a response to the question, 'What sort of person should I be and how should I live my life?' while morality is an answer to the question, 'What are my duties and responsibilities to others (and perhaps myself too, on some views)?' One's morality flows from one's ethics, and reciprocally influences its character; but its scope is narrower. As a vital constituent of the good in a life that is good, friendship is accordingly a matter of ethics. This means not only that the good life needs friendship in it, but therefore – as noted above – that two of the key ethical endeavours in it are reflections on how to be a good friend to one's friends and others, and how to know a good friend to oneself. The distinction turns on being a friend as an agent, and being befriended as a patient. In the 'real friend' nexus a necessary condition is that the parties are both of these things to each other – the mutuality condition – although here too it would be a mistake to ask for pure symmetry or equality, because at different times and in different ways the parties will surely be these things to each other in different degrees.

But there is an interesting catch to the idea of being a friend – the agency half of the equation – where this can be general-ised. In the examples and discussions canvassed in Part I above, it was an implication that *agape* is not friendship, because it does not discriminate or prefer one or some people over others, but is intended to be universal. This is the ideal of Christian charity (Latin *caritas* is the Greek *agape*). It is a comment on human nature and institutions that these words and the lovely ideas associated with them should have given eventual rise to the proverbial phrase 'as cold as charity'; but there it is. The thought now is that whereas being a 'real friend' to another *necessarily* assumes reciprocity and mutuality, 'being a friend' need not; if we said that the Good Samaritan befriended the man who fell among thieves, or 'was a friend to' that man, we would not be misusing the terms. On the contrary the office of friend is very much performed by the Samaritan, and it captures the idea well of what it would be for anyone to take the part of a friend to another who needed it – or indeed to anyone else in general, even in passing, even for a moment.[1]

The sense of obligation one might have in order to be involved in human rights activism, in campaigns for social justice, in movements for the liberation of the human mind and person, in working for more tolerant, generous and humane legal and social dispensations, in engagement in charitable work, would on this view be the outcome of taking a stance of friendship towards humanity. I see no reason not to go further and say: why cannot one be a friend to animals in opposing factory farming and other forms of cruelty, or a friend to the environment and through its protection to future generations? This is not to stretch the term one whit, because what is implicated in the general idea of being a friend to X, whoever or whatever X is, is the set of more particular ideas about concern, sympathy, interest, action towards the welfare of, and preparedness to sacrifice something of one's own substance or convenience for, that person or object.

Now there is no question but that engagement in an agency of friendship towards these general beneficiaries contributes to the satisfaction of life. Put simply, it feels good to do good. So as an ethical ideal, friendship merits being taken in this large sense too, and is at one with the universalism in many ethical outlooks (among which, for inclusiveness, the likes of Buddhism and Jainism stand out).

At the same time, the central notion of friendship remains the close mutual personal link between two or a very few people. Whereas it does not take much to see what being a friend to, say, the environment involves, personal friendship demands a great deal more thought, because it requires a degree of knowledge and understanding – two different things – of the other, sufficient to make one's agency towards him or her apt.

It also involves understanding what one is in for, so to speak, though not in a reductive or calculating sense; accepting, tolerating and sympathising with a friend involves a grasp of their failings and hopes – including the unrealistic ones – because one has to be at times ready to deal with them, just as one hopes one's friend or friends will cope with one's own.

It has been well said that we do not love our friends for their achievements, but (in part anyway) for what they want to achieve. A person's sincere aspirations say much about them, as do their efforts, and even if they do not quite get there in the end one can honour them for wishing to, and can love them for trying.

The second thought offered above as a surprising one is that friendship, as the desired terminus of all relationships, trumps other relationships. By this I mean that if friendship is so high a value – and reason and the consensus agree that it is – then it is a top-down, that is, it tells us what and how to value anything that leads to it or results in it. Another and yet more tendentious way of saying this is that friendship's high value implies that any conventions and constraints that prevent it or interfere with it are wrong. And it happens that there are many such in our contemporary society, as there have been – ringing the changes on what some of them are – throughout history.

In devil's advocacy I put the point at its most challenging by offering this for discussion: one constant in the way of barriers to friendship is sex. Sex is a controlled substance in almost all societies, with strict customs, morals and laws regulating when, where, with whom and in what circumstances it can happen. Monogamous sexual fidelity is the norm of expectation in Christian and Jewish societies, more honoured in the breach than in the observance because human nature, with its underlying biology, is not good at observing historically conditioned changes in customs and laws.

In fact it is not just sex itself but anything to do with it – pictures, words, naked bodies or body parts – that falls under the custom, morals and laws barricading it in, buttoning it up, hiding it away and repressing it as much as possible.[2] The result of organising anything to do with sex in these ways is that all other human contact and interaction is controlled. Take the example of a woman once she has settled into a domestic partnership such as marriage. She is thereafter supposed to restrict not just her sexual life but her emotional intimacy to one man, even though she might continue to have emotional intimacy (but generally not with a physical aspect) with one or a few women friends. She can have male friends, but there is a limit to how close she can be to them and in what ways. Everyone knows that as the domestic partnership passes through the years, it will change; it might and in the best cases it will deepen, and mature love will emerge from it; but as it changes, and as she does, she is still bound by the original contract of exclusivity in the kinds of relationships she can have outside it. She cannot love again, except at the risk of destroying the complex structure of the domestic project that arose from its origin.

Society, in its keenness to control and limit the kinds of affections and intimacies, contacts and mutualities, that people can have with one another, exacts a high cost for anyone in breach of its rules. Suppose the woman of our example becomes too friendly with a man other than her husband; suppose this friendship takes its natural course of hugging and close contact, kissing, perhaps even sexual congress, and this is found out; a too-likely cost is the break-up of a family unit – a massive penalty for a natural and – in itself, disentangled from all the corrugated-iron stacked around it in the ways of those customs, laws and expectations – a good thing. It will happen because her partner has been taught to think that she has committed a great wrong against him, the one who should be the exclusive owner of her affection and its expressions.

Of course the destruction envisaged here is the overblown penalty that our conventions exact for sexual infidelity mainly, but the point is that everything in the neighbourhood of this is affected by it – and this includes almost all friendships across the sexes, across ethnicities, across religious divides, across differences of age, all of them under the gaze of the moralising and controlling suspicious eye.

But if friendship is a great and high good, and if it can be, or can coexist with, or lead to, or arise from, neighbouring forms of closeness, intimacy and mutuality between people, then the customs and laws, moral or otherwise, which stand in its way are wrong.

An alternative view, which is the one that is actually operative, is of course to say that *only certain types* of friendship are acceptable. Most societies in their different conventional ways extend social acceptance only to these or those types of friendship, and this is perhaps why the commonplace vaunting of friendship that they also all go in for is so superficial. In its turn, that is why the thoughts prompted by the idea that friendship is a great ethical value are, when inspected, so surprising – because they are no longer intuitive.

One question which some might think is begged in the foregoing relates to the ambiguous and complex matter several times alluded to already: the matter of friendships across the gender divide. Are they really possible? Of course the question relates to men and women in the courting age and that part of adulthood where sexual interest might be aroused by propinquity or intimacy; no one thinks this of the very young or the very old, where it is perfectly obvious that such friendships are common.

There are at least two assumptions embedded here. One is that if a relationship is sexual, it is not a friendship. This is an assumption denied in passing often enough in the foregoing. The other is that if a relationship is a friendship, it is not sexual. 'We are just good friends,' a publicity-shy celebrity couple might say when speculation arises because they are seen together often; they are trading on this second assumption.

If one thinks that there is a distinction without a difference here, consider: many relationships begin as attractions, and develop into romantic affairs, these days usually with physical intimacy as a standard and significant part of them. As the couple come to know and depend upon each other more, still with the attraction and sexual elements central, they come to have the very features of a relationship which define friendship. Even the most energetic of lovers in the honeymoon phase might pause to eat or take a walk or have a conversation: in those intervals what connects them is what connects friends. Why not accept that they are friends too? Of course the 'too' is important: they are not *only* friends; and it is true that generally the term is reserved for the *only* case. But it need not be, and when it is said of lovers that they are good friends too, the implication is that they are (as the phrase has it) good together.

And looking at the relationship from the other end, we note that the reason for thinking that if 'they are friends' is an accurate description of the relationship subsisting between a couple or among a group, it is because we intend to convey the *only* sense. An interest in who is connected with whom and in what ways is a lively social one – studies of troops of baboons show that they evidence an elaborate knowledge of who is what to whom, because the different connections between kin and associates are integral to the troop's well-being, even survival. Human beings gossip for a deep reason: information about the shifting patterns of social relationships is significant in ways parallel to other primates (social survival might be the ultimate objective in the human case, but failing to survive socially is a kind of death). So the terminology marks a significant distinction, but we know that it can be a mask as well. The pragmatics of language play a role here: 'friend' said with a faint inflection of an eyebrow or a minute emphasis of tone removes the *only*.

There are relatively few cases where subjective personal experience is the right route to understanding a concept, but this is one of them. Or at least, it is part of what goes into understanding it. According to certain views, there are fundamental concepts in the architecture of our thought which are 'primitive' or basic in the sense that they cannot be explained, or explained adequately, other than by direct experience of their referents. Most concepts are such that direct experience of their referents is impossible: the concept 'the height of Mount Everest' is one that we grasp through understanding words, and the concept of an electron in particle physics is one that can only be grasped fully with the mathematical apparatus used to describe quantum phenomena. But one cannot adequately convey the meaning of 'yellow' unless at some point one can display a focal sample of that colour; or 'sweet', as applied to the sense of taste, without offering a sample of sugar or honey or some other substance which provokes that taste.

For each of us individually and therefore differently, the association of 'friend' will have the equivalent somewhere of a colour patch or a spoon of honey in personal experience. It will also have cinematic and literary associations, and in some ways these might be more powerful. Among my contemporaries at the age of eleven or so, William Brown and Ginger, with Douglas and Henry in tow, provided something of a model of what a gang of friends might be; more tamely, so did Julian, Dick, George and Anne with Timmy the dog.[3] We might have emulated them in our doings rather than understood their doings by extrapolating from our own case. Either way, personal experience of enacting friendship was being garnered.

Over the course of the years between the ages of eight and twelve I had four friends, not all of them at the same time or place, with whom I spent a lot of time, playing and making things, being cowboys and Indians, climbing trees, cycling about, and getting into mischief, all in the normal way. I was entirely unconscious of whatever it was that made me like them. I scarcely knew that I did – though I knew it when I did not like a boy: if I disliked a boy it was usually someone older who bullied or was in any other way unpleasant. To boys who were not friends I was indifferent or, more accurately, neutral; with my friends I and they simply assumed that we shared our interests.

One of these boys became a friend after we had encountered each other in a lane that divided the backs of our gardens, and a bristling stand-off resulted in which we averred that our respective big brothers could beat the other's big brother in a fight any day. We went and fetched our bemused big brothers to set them on one another, and the big brothers spoke in the friendliest fashion to each other, each gave his younger brother a cuff on the head, and they parted on good terms. The failure of our enterprise was very bonding. There was never an occasion when we decided to be friends; one of us said something like 'come and see my train set', and we scampered off, and thereafter during school holidays were forever in one another's homes or roaming about in boyish avocations.

The natural and instinctive bond at work is reflected in a phenomenon I observe in my dog. She is disdainful of most other dogs she meets while busy sniffing about in the park (the canine equivalent of checking emails, I often think), but occasionally will see another dog, even in the distance, and though to my knowledge not having encountered it before, will bound off in excitement to greet and play with it. No sense of smell is involved at that distance, so it is hard to know what triggers the response; someone wiser in dog ways might have a guess at the answer.

When I was a child there was one boy I know I liked because he was clever and interesting, very knowledgeable about dinosaurs and other arcana, and had a good collection of books. The son of a widowed mother who was rather protective of him, he had a head too large for his body – overloaded with brains, we were all confidently sure – with a shock of red hair curling all about it. Other boys disliked him for being smart and much cherished by the teachers, who I think were even a little nervous of him because although aged only about ten he was better at mathematics than they. Other boys were contemptuous of his contempt for sports. I found him entertaining and interesting, so I befriended him.

In the demanding and busy atmosphere of a boarding school, in days crowded with noise and effort, it was still possible to find oneself more in sympathy with certain boys than others, but it was rare that one could talk in the spontaneous way that allows confidences to be exchanged and real insight into the other to grow. Perhaps that circumstance was an artefact of the school's ethos – rather like those Victorian boarding schools anxious about the growth of homosexual feeling, it made every day a race to exhaustion. Reading accounts of life in the army, in barracks, even on campaign, is very reminiscent of that form of boarding-school regime, where comradeship emerged from a shared experience rather than friendship from mutual encounter. That is an interesting lesson.

My experience of friendship fully recognised as such, and reflected upon while it happened, first comes sharply into focus in the very last years of school, and in undergraduate life. In the latter, in particular, I enjoyed close friendships with two others, each of us very different from the others in external respects (social background principally) but with a similar sense of humour and – between the closest two of us – a range of shared reference in music and books that formed the basis of a short-hand way of talking. For our second and third undergraduate years we three shared a cottage in a narrow back street, cold and scarcely habitable, always untidy, but full of fun.

One of my two friends was diagnosed with cancer in his final year, and died a year later. I had come to know his family, and had grown close to his sister, before his illness; in the year of his dying, and in the days leading to his death, I witnessed the indescribable suffering of his parents, especially his father, for whom he was the proudest and most cherished fact of their lives, and to whom his death seemed to make the world a thing of incomprehensible stupidity for taking away something so young, bright and beautiful. My other friend had been the closer of the two, but now that the third had gone there was a sudden loosening of that bond. Of the three of us he had been the one to experiment with drugs, and they had begun to take a toll. He was very clever, but the drugs seemed to be ruining his mind; he was foolish under their influence, and tiresome; it was deeply dismaying. As with the other lost friend, it seemed that something else was moving the tectonic plates beneath our feet, distancing us against our power or will, making us irrelevant to each other.

Perhaps the richest experience of friendship came subsequently, when married life began, and the friendships then formed were as one of a couple with other married couples who had, as we did, young children. Here there were substantial similarities and shared experiences, opportunities for helping each other – mutual babysitting, taking the kids to school, playing bridge because we could not go out as much as when we were single and childless. These were opportunities for getting to know others in more extensive and fuller ways that combined the practical and the personal. And there were of course real problems to deal with – the illness or accidents that affected children, the occasional separation or divorce involving one of the couples in the circle, the adulteries within it or outside it: the texture of actual as opposed to virtual life and the weight of responsibility we variously felt, made friendships deeper. These were friendships that exemplified the features celebrated in the idealised and the sensible versions:

the mutuality, sharing of information, time, resources such as infants' clothing handed on, the reciprocated help, the understanding and forgiveness of others who knew one so well that one did not have to repeat an explanation every time one was due.

And with the accumulation of time since, some of those friendships have matured into the kind that do not need to be furbished on a frequent basis, but can be picked up and set down even at the distance of years without a single beat being missed in the rhythms that underlie them. They still exemplify the central features of friendship, as one sees when asked: would you get out of bed and go in the middle of the night across country to a friend if they had a sudden urgent need of you? The answer is Yes; how could one not? It would be an honour to answer the call of a friend; to make a sacrifice of something so minor, in the circumstances of a request for help, as one's sleep or time would be nothing – you would do more if you could, or if it were needed.

Some people have a talent for friendship, others less so; but the value of friendship to someone who has only one or a very few friends whom they see only occasionally is no different from what it is for someone who has a wide circle of acquaintance among whom a few come in and out of focus as specially close for a time. In both cases the fact is that there is one or more others in whose company, or even in thoughts of whom, there is something that lies on a significant side of the border we set around ourselves to demarcate where the rest of the world begins; and who therefore have a claim, and constitute a possession, which we could be without only at the great cost of making the world a far poorer place.

We might conclude on the strange note that we never call a friend 'friend'. 'Friend, would you like a cup of tea?' is something we might say to a stranger when serving at a village fete. When the presenter on the television programme addresses the children presumed to be sitting at home watching, she might say 'Hello my friends!' but she does not know a single one of them personally. In fact if you call someone 'friend' to his or her face you might very well be feeling rather unfriendly towards them – 'You watch out my friend, any more of that and I'll punch you on the nose!'

The situations in which we use 'friend' are when we talk of absent parties, or when we qualify the word as in 'girlfriend' and 'boyfriend', as we might when introducing the specified person, and therefore in that person's presence. But we would only do so with permission, because to give someone that title presumes a great deal which has to have been given and accepted beforehand.

But if we do use 'friend' in addressing a friend, it is a mark that there is something wrong in the offing. We are advising, exhorting, warning, pleading; we remind the friend that we are a friend, that we have the licence to do what we are doing or to say what we are saying which is given by friendship. Or perhaps it is at the end of friendship, or in a conversation when the despairing realisation that the loss of friendship has occurred, that we invoke the term and its power in hope of revival or perhaps in acceptance of farewell.

Romances which are not destined to start because of one person's reluctance, or which have come to an end, turn on the sharp point of the word, now occurring in a bleak guise: 'I like you as a friend,' says the girl repelling the amorous boy;

'let's always be friends,' says the Lothario to the discarded maiden.

One hears people use the formula 'friend of mine', which is often a redundancy; 'A friend told me' says the same thing as 'a friend of mine told me'. It would be pointful to say 'a friend of X's' in order to discriminate between someone else's friend and one's own. But the formula has stuck. It is nevertheless an interesting one in its emphasis on the possessive: 'my friend', 'a friend of mine'; a friend belongs to me and I belong to him; that is part of what feels good about it.

Friendship in the personal sphere is valued and desired. In the political sphere it is regarded with suspicion at times, because it provokes anxieties that the loyalties involved might serve hidden and private interests and not those of office. In business, friendships are important; people cultivate friends and connections because they bring definite advantages which are most valued when mutual so, unless deceit enters, such friendships are a productive thing. We might hope that friendships in any sphere of life are welcome, for Aristotle's reason that a society is the better for the amities and concords that friendship creates among people, so that if the society were a great nexus of good fellowship, it would be one where individual and collective *eudaimonia* would exist.

Yet we limit the opportunity for friendships in too many cases; the boundaries between genders, ages, religions, ethnicities, roles and offices all bring down the shutters on personal relations because of the assumed – and, to be fair, sometimes real – dangers that might arise from their abuse. It could be argued that in the interests of an Aristotelian 'society of friends' (not the Quakers) project, the default should be to start with a presumption in favour of friendship. That would not be so far-fetched; in earlier pages it was acknowledged that the essentially social nature of human beings predisposes to friendship, and in fact we have to work rather hard to put obstacles in the way of it, especially among the young. Children in a kindergarten will unconsciously be friends with anyone at all, of any persuasion, background, colour, faith or political family; it is society – that is: it is we who – create the friendship-dismantling mechanisms of division and difference.

In the end, though, it is personal friendship which is the central point in this discussion. I repeat what I said at the outset: we regard it as a success if we become friends with our parents when we grow up, our children when they grow up, our lovers and spouses and workmates even when they remain lovers and spouses and workmates – for in every case a bond comes to exist, and can be relied on, which transcends the other reasons we entered into association with the people in question. Those bonds are a large part of what gives meaning to our lives, just as our lives give meaning to them: without them we are less, and in danger of being too close to nothing.

Notes

Introduction

1. Vera Brittain, *Testament of Friendship*, p. 2.
2. Ibid. p. 10.

1 The *Lysis* and *Symposium*

1. *Lysis* 210 e, *The Dialogues of Plato*, Vol. 2 trans. Benjamin Jowett in 'The *Symposium* and Other Dialogues' 3rd edn, 1924.
2. Ibid. 207 c.
3. *Charmides* 154 e Jowett op. cit.
4. *Lysis* 210 c, d.
5. Ibid. 211 e.
6. Ibid. 212–13 b.
7. Ibid. 214 e.
8. Ibid. 215 a.
9. Ibid. 215 a, b.
10. Ibid. 222 e.
11. Ibid. 223 b.
12. Ibid. 221 d, e.
13. Aristotle *Nicomachean Ethics*, trans. Sarah Brodie and Christopher Rowe, Oxford: Oxford University Press, 2002, 1155a5–10.

2 The Classic Statement: Aristotle

1. Aristotle, *Nicomachean Ethics*, 1155a15.
2. Ibid. 1144a25.
3. Aristotle, *Politics* 1295b23–5.
4. Ibid. 1280b38–9.
5. *Nicomachean Ethics*, 1155b21–7.
6. Ibid. 1155a10–15.
7. Ibid. 1155b1–10.
8. Ibid. 1156a6–b10.
9. Ibid. 1156a20–25.
10. Ibid. 1156b–1.
11. Ibid. 1156b5–15.
12. Ibid. 1156a35.
13. Ibid. 1166b30 et. seq.
14. Ibid. 1166a31–2.
15. Ibid. 1166a12–20.
16. Ibid. 1166a1–28.
17. Ibid. 1094b7–10.
18. Ibid. 1094a1–3.
19. Ibid. 1098a16–17.
20. This tripartite distinction is reminiscent of what Pythagoras had long before said about the three types of people: those who come to participate in the Games, those who come to watch the Games, and those who come to buy and sell under the stands: the practical, the contemplative, and the banausic.

3 Cicero *De amicitia*

1. Cicero *De amicitia* iv.18.
2. W. A. Falconer *Cicero*, Vol. XX Loeb Classical Library, London, 1929, p. 106.
3. Cicero *De amicitia* iv.15.
4. Ibid. iv.18.
5. Ibid. iv.19.
6. Ibid. iv.19–20.
7. Ibid. vi.20.
8. Ibid. vi.21.
9. Ibid. vi.22.
10. Ibid.
11. Ibid. vii.23.
12. Ibid. vii.24.

13. Ibid. viii.26.
14. Ibid. viii.27.
15. Ibid. Ix.30–1.
16. Ibid.
17. Ibid. x.35.
18. E. M. Forster *Two Cheers for Democracy*, London: Edward Arnold & Co., 1951, p. 78.
19. *De amicitia* xi.37. Cicero is writing about contemporary as much as past events here: the usurpation of the Republic by Caesar was a very recent event from which he had personally suffered.
20. Ibid. xii.40.
21. Ibid. xiii.44.
22. Ibid. xiii.45–6.
23. Ibid. xiii.48.
24. Ibid. xv.52–3.
25. Ibid. xvi.57.
26. Ibid. xvi.58.
27. Ibid. xvi.59.
28. Ibid. xvii.61.
29. Ibid. xviii.65.
30. Ibid. xvii.63.
31. Ibid. xvii.64.
32. Ibid. xviii.66.
33. Ibid. xxii.82.
34. Ibid. xxi.80.
35. Plutarch 'On the Abundance of Friends,' in *Moral Essays* trans. A. R. Shilleto, London, 1898. The essay is more often cited (by Montaigne and others) as 'On the Plurality of Friends'.
36. Ibid. p. 146.
37. Ibid. p. 147.
38. Ibid.
39. Ibid. 148.
40. Ibid. 149.
41. Ibid. 150.
42. Ibid. 149.
43. Ibid. 150.
44. Ibid. 154.

4 Christianity and Friendship

1. Augustine *Confessions* III 56–7, trans. E. B. Pusey Dent, London, 1966.

2. Augustine *City of God* 447, trans. M. Dods, Peabody, MA: Hendrickson Publishers, 2009.

3. *Confessions* IV.7.

4. Ibid.

5. Ibid. IV.9.

6. Ibid. IV.13.

7. Ibid. IV.14.

8. Ibid. IV.20.

9. Ibid. IV.14.

10. The Gospel According to St Luke 10: 25–37.

11. *The Letters of Abélard and Héloïse*, London: Penguin, 2004, *passim*.

12. Augustine *Letter to Jerome* 394 CE http://www.newadvent.org/fathers/1102.htm.

13. Augustine *Sermon* 16.

14. Ibid. 385.

15. Augustine *Letter* 130.

16. Augustine *Confessions* V.19.

17. Ibid. II.5.

18. Ibid. II.4.

19. Augustine *Letter* 258.

20. Ibid.

21. Ibid. 192.

22. Cited above, p. 64.

23. Aquinas *Summa theologica* I–II q. 4.

24. Ibid.

25. Ibid. II–II q 153–5.

26. Ibid. II–II q 170–1.

27. Ibid. II–II q 26.

28. Ibid. q 172.

29. Ibid. q 180.

30. Aquinas *De caritate* 7. 9.

31. Aquinas *Summa Theologica* II–II q 176.

32. Bertrand Russell *History of Western Philosophy* London 1967 edn, p. 463.

33. For example, http://www.fusion101.com/guide/christian-friendship.htm

5 Renaissance Friendship

1. According to Frazer in *The Golden Bough*, the Virgin Mary is the successor to the virgin goddess Diana, worshipped at Aricia near

Lake Nemi. Because of the devotion to Diana at this holy place, the early Church had a problem weaning Diana's epigones away; and therefore announced that Diana's real name was Mary (etc.). See Sir James Frazer, *The Golden Bough* XVI; also 'Certainly in art the figure of Isis suckling the infant Horus is so like that of the Madonna and child that it has sometimes received the adoration of ignorant Christians': ibid. XLI.

2. Munich's Alte Pinakothek is a repository of some remarkable examples of the minatory and coercive art of medieval Christendom in this line.

3. Giovanni Boccaccio *The Decameron of Giovanni Boccaccio*, trans. John Payne, New York, NY: Random House, p. 502.

4. A justification for this remark occurs in the final part of this book.

5. Christopher Marlow. 'Friendship in Renaissance England', *Literature Compass*, 1, 1 (2003–4).

6. There is an excellent survey of these sources in Laurie Shannon *Sovereign Amity: Figures of Friendship in Shakespearian Contexts*, Chicago: Chicago University Press, 2002, pp. 3 et seq.

7. Desiderius Erasmus *The Colloquies*, Vol. 2, 1518, Ephorinus to John.

8. All quoted in Shannon *Sovereign Amity*, pp. 3–4.

9. Ibid. pp. 5–6.

10. Ibid. p. 7.

11. By far the best translation of Montaigne is the one by M. A. Screech, *Michel de Montaigne: The Complete Essays* (Harmondsworth: Penguin Classics new edn, 1993); not just the best, but superb. For greater ease of reference I use the very adequate Cohen translation, made earlier for Penguin Classics, *Michel de Montaigne Essays* (1958), which more readers are likely to have to hand, as it is a selection. Again for ease of reference, I use an edition of Bacon's *Essays* that appears free online, at http://www.literaturepage.com/read/francis-bacon-essays-54.html.

12. Montaigne *Essays*, ed. p. 254.

13. Ibid. p. 253.

14. Ibid.

15. Ibid. p. 254.

16. Ibid. p. 257.

17. Ibid.

18. Ibid. p. 255.

19. Ibid. p. 257.

20. Ibid. p. 258.

21. Ibid. p. 261.
22. Ibid. p. 90.
23. Ibid. p. 97.
24. Ibid. pp. 97–8.
25. Ibid. pp. 98–9.
26. Ibid. p. 99.
27. Ibid. p. 92.
28. Ibid. p. 93.
29. Ibid.
30. Ibid.
31. Ibid. p. 94.
32. Ibid. p. 96.
33. Francis Bacon, *Essays* Harvard Classics, Vol. 3, p. 54 Cambridge, MA: Harvard University Press, 1910–14.
34. Ibid.
35. Ibid. p. 55.
36. Ibid. p. 56.
37. Ibid. p. 57.
38. Ibid.
39. Ibid. p. 58.
40. Ibid. p. 59.
41. Ibid.

6 From Enlightenment back to the Roman Republic

1. Death was not the worst penalty, though; leaving aside the hideous tortures to which heretics, 'witches' and others were subjected, it was asserted that the ecclesiastical powers on earth had the ability to prevent someone from ever getting into heaven, by excommunicating him; for 'there is no salvation outside the Church', and to be shut out from it and not to repent and beg for readmission was to be shut out of felicity for eternity.
2. Immanuel Kant '*What is Enlightenment?* 1784. (At the end of the original, Kant signed his name and put 'Königsberg in Prussia, 30 September 1784).
3. Kant *Lectures on Ethics*. The standard way of referencing these is through the sets of notes from which they come; the references to follow will direct the close scholar, should there be one, of these words. R15: 321, L.E. Collins 27: 422.
4. Ibid. LE Collins 27: 422–3.
5. Ibid. R15:624.
6. Ibid. LE Collins 27: 424–5.

7. Ibid. LE Collins 27:426.

8. Ibid. LE Collins 27: 427, adjusting 'we' to 'he'.

9. Ibid. LE Vigilantius 27: 676.

10. Immanuel Kant *The Groundwork of the Metaphysic of Morals*, trans. H. J. Paton, London: Hutchinson, 1948.

11. Ibid. 6: 470.

12. Ibid. 6: 471.

13. Ibid.

14. Kant's moral philosophy is set out in *The Groundwork of the Metaphysics of Morals* (1785), *The Critique of Practical Reason* (1788) and *The Metaphysics of Morals* (1796).

15. David Hume. See Book II of *A Treatise of Human Nature* (1740) 'Of the Passions' *passim*, and An *Enquiry into the Principles of Morals* (1751). A source of this sceptical view about the motivating efficacy of reason is Pyrrhonian scepticism.

16. This is a loose rendering of the 'categorical imperative' *Groundwork of the Metaphysics of Morals* 30.

17. See Antonio R. Damasio *Descartes' Error: Emotion, Reason, and the Human Brain*, New York, NY: Putnam's Sons, 1994.

18. The brilliant Emilie marquise du Châtelet was a mathematician and physicist famous among other things for translating Newton's *Principia* into French, a translation that is still in use today.

19. Adam Smith; the relevant texts are *The Wealth of Nations* (1776) and *The Theory of Moral Sentiments* (1759).

20. Smith *Moral Sentiments* VI 12–13, 222–3.

21. Smith *Wealth of Nations* I.ii.1, 25.

22. David Hume *Essays Moral, Political and Literary* 1777: 'Of the Jealousy of Trade'.

23. See A. Silver 'Friendship in Commercial Society: Eighteenth-Century Social Theory and Modern Sociology', *European Journal of Sociology* 95: 1474–504.

24. Adam Smith *The Wealth of Nations*, Chicago, IL: University of Chicago Press, 1977, p. 747.

25. Smith *Moral Sentiments* II.3.

26. Hume *Treatise of Human Nature* (1740).

27. Henry Fielding *The History of Tom Jones*, 242.

28. Ibid. 779.

29. William Hazlitt *The Spirit of the Age* 'William Godwin', 1825.

30. William Godwin *Thoughts on Man: His Nature, Productions and Discoveries, Interspersed with some Particulares respecting the Author*, London: 'Essay XV Of Love and Friendship', 1831. All

references are to an unpaginated ebook provided by the University of Adelaide, Australia, at http://ebooks.adelaide.edu.au/g/godwin/william/thoughts/chapter15.html.

31. Ibid.
32. inid.
33. Ibid.
34. Ibid.
35. Ibid.
36. Ibid.
37. Ibid.
38. Ibid.
39. Ibid.
40. The assumption of unstated but undying loyalty to a friend which is the premise of the sidekick theme is what makes the following joke about the Lone Ranger and Tonto so funny: the two suddenly find themselves surrounded by hostile Sioux or Cheyenne; the Lone Ranger says, 'Tonto! We're surrounded by Indians!' whereupon Tonto replies, '*We*, Kemo Sabe?'. Tonto was an Indian.
41. Some of the information here comes very helpfully from interesting work by LaMont L. Egle 'Plotting Friendship: Male Bonds in Early Nineteenth-Century British Fiction', PhD dissertation University of Michigan, 2009. It directed me to some reading I would not otherwise have done.
42. Thomas Hughes *Tom Brown's Schooldays* 1857, p. 182.
43. Thomas Hughes *Tom Brown at Oxford* 1861, p. 73.
44. Quoted in C. Oulton *Romantic Friendship in Victorian Literature*, Aldershot: Ashgate, 2007, p. 39.
45. Some speaking nineteenth-century photographs of the subject can be viewed at http://artofmanliness.com/2008/08/24/the-history-and-nature-of-man-friendships/
46. Stendhal *De L'Amour* tells of the 'Salzburg bough', the little twig dangled down the salt mine until glittering with crystals, and presented to the object of one's infatuation as a love token; the idea is that we cover the other in a disguise of brilliancies, which only melt away when the quiet of the marriage-bed has replaced the hurly-burly of the chaise longue (to use Mrs Patrick Campbell's immortal phrase).
47. Since Edvard Westermarck's *History of Human Marriage* (1903; quite what 'human' is doing in the title is obscure) and most particularly since the liberalisation of divorce laws, the not exclusively anthropological literature on marriage has burgeoned

exponentially; most of it is of the exhortatory or self-help type, and comprehensive studies are relatively few because of the complexity and diversity of the subject. Studies of family life, being wider in focus, are more helpful in general to understanding the importance of the bonds that lie at the heart of our social lives.

48. At the time of writing, the movement for the gay right to marry, not merely to enter 'civil partnerships', is in full flow in the UK and the US, marking a desire for integration into social normality.

7 Excursus: Friendship Illustrated

1. Plutarch tells us in his life of Pericles that Pericles kissed Aspasia every day, both on leaving home and on returning to it. This was regarded as extraordinary behaviour between a man and a woman at that time, and hence worth remarking.
2. Homer *The Iliad* Book IX.
3. Aeschylus fragments 135, 136, Plato *Symposium* 179e–180b; Aeschines *Timarchus* 133, 141 et seq.
4. The Iliad Book XI.
5. Ibid. Book XV.
6. Ibid. Book XVI.
7. Ibid. Book XVII.
8. Ibid.
9. Ibid.
10. Ibid.
11. Ibid. Book XVIII.
12. Ibid.
13. Ibid.
14. Ibid.
15. Ibid. Book XXII.
16. Ibid. Book XXIII.
17. Ibid. Book XXIV.
18. 1 Samuel 15.
19. 1 Samuel 16.
20. Ibid.
21. Ibid. 18. Either Saul was particularly forgetful or the Bible's frequent editorial problems are evident here: this chapter has Saul and David meeting for the first time despite David's soothing of Saul with the lyre in the previous chapter.
22. Ibid. 18.
23. Ibid.

24. Ibid. 19.
25. Ibid. 20.
26. Ibid.
27. 2 Samuel 1.
28. It is instructive to look at the missionary literature on these matters on the internet: http://pleaseconvinceme.com/2012/were-david-and-jonathan-homosexual-lovers/
29. See W. R. Childs (ed.) *Vita Edwardi Secundi*, Oxford: Oxford University Press, 2005.
30. Roger of Hoveden *Annals*, trans. H. T. Riley, London, 1853 Vol. II, pp. 63–4.
31. Ibid. p. 356.
32. Ruth 1:8–9.
33. Ibid. 1:16–17.
34. See A. Brenner (ed.) *Ruth and Esther: A Feminist Companion to the Bible*, Sheffield: University of Sheffield Press, 1999; M. D. Coogan, *A Brief Introduction to the Old Testament*, Oxford: Oxford University Press, 2009.
35. See Genesis 2:24, Ruth 1:14. This point is asserted in campaigns for equal marriage rights for gay and lesbian people; see, for example, http://www.wouldjesusdiscriminate.org/biblical_evidence/ruth_naomi.html.
36. *Iliad* Book IV.
37. Themistius, *Private Orations*, trans. R. J. Penella, Berkeley, CA: University of California Press, 2000, p. 95.
38. Ibid. pp. 89–90.
39. Ibid. pp. 91–3.
40. Ibid. pp. 93–4.
41. Ibid. p. 94.
42. Ibid. p. 95.
43. Ibid. pp. 97–9.
44. Ibid. pp. 99–100.
45. Virgil *The Aeneid* Book IX.
46. Ibid.
47. Ibid.
48. Ibid.
49. Ibid. Book V.
50. Lucian *Amores*, trans. W. J. Baylis.
51. Ibid., slightly adapted for style.
52. S. Guy-Bray *Loving in Verse: Poetic Influence as Erotic*, Toronto: University of Toronto Press, 2006 p. 51.

53. See the entry in James Lewis Thomas Chalmers Spence *A Dictionary of Medieval Romance Writers,* London: George Routledge & Sons, 1913.
54. Guy-Bray *Loving* p. 52.
55. *The Book of Good Counsels* (from the *Hitopadesa*) trans. Sir Edwin Arnold Smith, London, Edler & Co., 1861, 'Story of the Vulture, the Cat, and the Birds'.
56. For a depiction of how this works see an image of the Attic red-figure vase in the Museum of Fine Arts, Boston, showing Zephyros and Hyakinthos *c.* 480 BCE, at http://www.theoi.com/Gallery/T29.1.html.
57. Genesis 38: 9–10.
58. Leviticus 20: 13.
59. Adam Sisman *The Friendship: Wordsworth and Coleridge,* London: Harperpress, 2006.
60. David Bodanis *Passionate Minds: The Great Enlightenment Love Affair,* London: Little, Brown, 2006.
61. Robert B. Silvers and Barbara Epstein (eds) *The Company They Kept: Writers on Unforgettable Friendships,* New York, NY: New York Review of Books, 2011.
62. C. Ricks *Tennyson,* London: Macmillan, 1972.

9 Friendship Examined

1. Anthony Price makes play of those in relation to his own twin brother in connection with Aristotle's remark. See *Love and Friendship in Plato and Aristotle,* Acknowledgements, Oxford: Clarendon Press, 1994.

10 The Two Claims

1. Luke 10:25–37.
2. Some historical contrasts are stark. Public nudity or exposure of genitals is regarded as 'indecent'. In ancient Sparta boys and girls exercised naked together in the gymnasium; *gymnos* means 'naked'. In England it is still illegal to show an image of an erect male penis. In ancient Rome depictions of erect male penises were placed over every front door, and worn as amulets on the arms of girls, to ward off the evil eye. Such is the way with customs and time.
3. These were respectively characters in Richmal Crompton's *Just William* stories, and the Famous Five of Enid Blyton.

Bibliography

Annas, J., 1977, 'Plato and Aristotle on Friendship and Altruism', *Mind*, 86: 532–54.

——, 1988, 'Self-Love in Aristotle', *Southern Journal of Philosophy*, Supp.7: 1–18.

Annis, D. B., 1987, 'The Meaning, Value, and Duties of Friendship', *American Philosophical Quarterly*, 24: 349–56.

Badhwar, N. K., 1987, 'Friends as Ends in Themselves', *Philosophy & Phenomenological Research*, 48: 1–23.

——, 1991, 'Why It Is Wrong to Be Always Guided by the Best: Consequentialism and Friendship', *Ethics*, 101: 483–504.

——, (ed.), 1993, *Friendship: A Philosophical Reader*, Ithaca, NY: Cornell University Press.

——, 2003, 'Love', in H. LaFollette (ed.), *Practical Ethics*, Oxford: Oxford University Press, 42–69.

Bech, Henning, 1997, *When Men Meet: Homosexuality and Modernity*, Chicago: Chicago University Press.

Bernstein, M., 2007, 'Friends without Favoritism', *Journal of Value Inquiry*, 41: 59–76.

Blum, L. A., 1980, *Friendship, Altruism, and Morality*, London: Routledge & Kegan Paul.

——, 1993, 'Friendship as a Moral Phenomenon', in Badhwar (1993), 192–210.

Bibliography

Bratman, M. E., 1999, *Faces of Intention: Selected Essays on Intention and Agency*, Cambridge: Cambridge University Press.

Brink, D. O., 1999, 'Eudaimonism, Love and Friendship, and Political Community', *Social Philosophy & Policy*, 16: 252–89.

Card, R. F., 2004, 'Consequentialism, Teleology, and the New Friendship Critique', *Pacific Philosophical Quarterly*, 85: 149–72.

Chaplin, Gregory, 2001, 'One Flesh One Heart One Soul: Renaissance Friendship and Miltonic Marriage' in *Modern Philology*, Chicago: Chicago University Press.

Cocking, D. and Kennett, J., 1998, 'Friendship and the Self', *Ethics*, 108: 502–27.

——, 2000, 'Friendship and Moral Danger', *Journal of Philosophy*, 97: 278–96.

——, and Oakley, J., 1995, 'Indirect Consequentialism, Friendship, and the Problem of Alienation', *Ethics*, 106: 86–111.

Conee, E., 2001, 'Friendship and Consequentialism', *Australasian Journal of Philosophy*, 79: 161–79.

Conger, John Janeway and Galambos, Nancy (1996), *Adolescence and Youth: Psychological Development in a Changing World*, London: Longman.

Cooper, J. M., 1977a, 'Aristotle on the Forms of Friendship', *Review of Metaphysics*, 30: 619–48.

——, 1977b, 'Friendship and the Good in Aristotle', *Philosophical Review*, 86: 290–315.

Friedman, M. A., 1989, 'Friendship and Moral Growth', *Journal of Value Inquiry*, 23: 3–13.

——, 1993, *What Are Friends For? Feminist Perspectives on Personal Relationships and Moral Theory*, Ithaca, NY: Cornell University Press.

——, 1998, 'Romantic Love and Personal Autonomy', *Midwest Studies in Philosophy*, 22: 162–81.

Gilbert, M., 1996, *Living Together: Rationality, Sociality, and Obligation*, Lanham, MD: Rowman & Littlefield.

——, 2000, *Sociality and Responsibility: New Essays in Plural Subject Theory*, Lanham, MD: Rowman & Littlefield.

——, 2006, *A Theory of Political Obligation: Membership, Commitment, and the Bonds of Society*, Oxford: Oxford University Press.

Grunebaum, J. O., 2005, 'Fair-Weather Friendships', *Journal of Value Inquiry*, 39: 203–14.

Bibliography

Helm, B., 2008, 'Plural Agents', *Noûs*, 42: 17–49.

Heyking, John von and Avramenko, Richard, 2008, *Friendship and Politics: Essays in Political Thought*, Notre Dame, IN: Notre Dame University Press.

Hoffman, E., 1997, 'Love as a Kind of Friendship', in *Sex, Love, and Friendship: Studies of the Society for the Philosophy of Sex and Love 1977–92*, Amsterdam: Rodopi, 109–19.

Hurka, T., 2006, 'Value and Friendship: A More Subtle View', *Utilitas*, 18: 232–42.

Jeske, D., 1997, 'Friendship, Virtue, and Impartiality', *Philosophy & Phenomenological Research*, 57: 51–72.

——, 2008, 'Friendship and the Grounds of Reasons', *Les Ateliers de l'Ethique*, 3: 61–9.

Kalmijn, Matthijs, 2002, 'Sex Segregation of Friendship Networks: Individual and Structural Determinants of Having Cross-Sex Friends', *European Sociological Review*, 18, 1 (March): 101–17.

Keller, S., 2000, 'How Do I Love Thee? Let Me Count the Properties', *American Philosophical Quarterly*, 37: 163–73.

Kent, Dale V., *Friendship, Love and Trust in Renaissance Florence*, Cambridge MA: Harvard University Press.

Lewis, C. S., 1974, *The Four Loves*, London: Collins.

Lynch, S., 2005, *Philosophy and Friendship*, Edinburgh: Edinburgh University Press.

Marlow, Christopher, 'Friendship in Renaissance England' (2003–4) *Literature Compass* 1, 1.

Mason, E., 1998, 'Can an Indirect Consequentialist Be a Real Friend?', *Ethics*, 108: 386–93.

Millgram, E., 1987, 'Aristotle on Making Other Selves', *Canadian Journal of Philosophy*, 17: 361–76.

Muraco, Anna, 2005, 'Heterosexual Evaluations of Hypothetical Friendship Behavior Based on Sex and Sexual Orientation', *Journal of Social and Personal Relationships*, 22, 5 (Oct.): 587–605.

Norton, Rictor (2008) 'Faithful Friend and Doting Lover', *The Homosexual Pastoral Tradition* <http://rictornorton.co.uk/pastor07.htm>

Nozick, R., 1989, 'Love's Bond', in *The Examined Life: Philosophical Meditations*, New York: Simon & Schuster, 68–86.

Price, A. W., 1994, *Love and Friendship in Plato and Aristotle*, Oxford: Clarendon Press.

Railton, P., 1984, 'Alienation, Consequentialism, and the Demands of Morality', *Philosophy & Public Affairs*, 13: 134–71.

Bibliography

Reeder, Heidi M., 2003, 'The Effect of Gender Role Orientation on Same and Cross-Sex Friendship Formation', *Sex Roles: A Journal of Research*, 49, 3–4, (Aug.): 143–52.

Rorty, A. O., 1986/1993, 'The Historicity of Psychological Attitudes: Love Is Not Love Which Alters Not When It Alteration Finds', in Badhwar (1993), 73–88.

Sadler, B., 2006, 'Love, Friendship, Morality', *Philosophical Forum*, 37: 243–63.

Scanlon, T. M., 1998, *What We Owe to Each Other*, Cambridge, MA: Harvard University Press.

Schoeman, F., 1985, 'Aristotle on the Good of Friendship', *Australasian Journal of Philosophy*, 63: 269–82.

Searle, J. R., 1990, 'Collective Intentions and Actions', in P. R. Cohen, M. E. Pollack and J. L. Morgan (eds), *Intentions in Communication*, Cambridge, MA: MIT Press, 401–15.

Shannon, Laurie, 2002, *Sovereign Amity: Figures of Friendship in Shakespearean Contexts*, Chicago: Chicago University Press.

Sherman, N., 1987, 'Aristotle on Friendship and the Shared Life', *Philosophy & Phenomenological Research*, 47: 589–613.

Stocker, M., 1976, 'The Schizophrenia of Modern Ethical Theories', *Journal of Philosophy*, 73: 453–66.

——, 1981, 'Values and Purposes: The Limits of Teleology and the Ends of Friendship', *Journal of Philosophy*, 78: 747–65.

Taylor, G., 1985, *Pride, Shame, and Guilt: Emotions of Self-Assessment*, Oxford: Oxford University Press.

Tedesco, M., 2006, 'Indirect Consequentialism, Suboptimality, and Friendship', *Pacific Philosophical Quarterly*, 87: 567–77.

Telfer, E., 1970–71, 'Friendship', *Proceedings of the Aristotelian Society*, 71: 223–41.

Thomas, L., 1987, 'Friendship', *Synthese*, 72: 217–36.

——, 1989, 'Friends and Lovers', in G. Graham and H. LaFollette (eds), *Person to Person*, Philadelphia, PA: Temple University Press, 182–98.

——, 1993, 'Friendship and Other Loves', in Badhwar (1993), 48–64.

Tuomela, R., 1995, *The Importance of Us: A Philosophical Study of Basic Social Notions*, Stanford, CA: Stanford University Press.

——, 2007, *The Philosophy of Sociality: The Shared Point of View*, Oxford: Oxford University Press.

Velleman, J. David, 1999, 'Love as a Moral Emotion', *Ethics*, 109: 338–74.

Bibliography

White, R. J., 1999a, 'Friendship: Ancient and Modern', *International Philosophical Quarterly*, 39: 19–34.

——, 1999b, 'Friendship and Commitment', *Journal of Value Inquiry*, 33: 79–88.

——, 2001, *Love's Philosophy*, Lanham, MD: Rowman & Littlefield.

Whiting, J. E., 1986, 'Friends and Future Selves', *Philosophical Review*, 95: 547–80.

——, 1991, 'Impersonal Friends', *Monist*, 74: 3–29.

Wilcox, W. H., 1987, 'Egoists, Consequentialists, and Their Friends', *Philosophy & Public Affairs*, 16: 73–84.

Williams, B., 1981, 'Persons, Character, and Morality', in *Moral Luck*, Cambridge: Cambridge University Press, 1–19.

Index

Index

Index

desire
  friendship and love in Plato's
    Symposium 26–7, 28–9
  sex and heterosexual
    friendships 101–2, 123–4,
    173–4, 179, 190–4
  see also homosexual love in
    history
Diana: Virgin Mary as successor
  to 206–7*n*
Dickens, Charles 113, 117
Diderot, René 95
Diomedes and Sthenelus 140–4
Disraeli, Benjamin: *Coningsby*
  113
divorce 2
dogs 196
Dorke, Walter: *A Tipe or Figure
  of Friendship* 80
durability of friendship
  157–8
duty and Kant's limits on
  friendship 99–100, 101

education
  boarding schools and
    'virtuous' male friendship
    114–16
  Empire and classical role
    models 112–17
Edward II, king of England 137
Egan, Pierce: *Life in London* and
  sequel 113
Einstein, Albert 160
Eliot, George 117, 162
Eliot, T. S. 162
Elyot, Thomas: *The Boke
  Named the Governor* 80
emotion 3–5
  and action 100, 108

Bacon on fruits of friendship
  91–2
Cicero on affection and
  friendship 46, 51, 56–7
and Hume's philosophy 100–1
Kant's objections 10, 99–100,
  101
role in life and reasoning 101
Stoics and reason 7–8
see also affection; love and
  friendship
Empire and classical role models
  111–17
empiricism 95–6
ending of friendship 157–9,
  179, 197
see also loss of friends
enemies and Christian doctrine
  68–9, 72
Enlightenment friendship
  95–119
Epicureans 6–7
Epicurus 7
Epstein, Barbara 159
Epstein, Jason 160
equality between friends 53, 98–9
  classical antiquity and
    inequality in friendship
    109–10, 126–7, 132
  problem of friendship with
    God 9, 70
  value and nature of
    inequalities in friendship
    51–2, 99, 107, 108–11
  see also mutual benefit;
    utilitarianism
Erasmus, Desiderius 42, 79–80
erotic attraction *see* desire;
  homosexual love in
  history; sex

Index

good of friendship in Plato's
Lysis 24–5
Goodman, Paul 161
goodness *see* virtue and
friendship
goodwill and friendship
Aristotle's view as component
33, 34
Cicero on 45, 46–7, 48, 51,
54–5, 56–7
Fielding's esteem of good-
heartedness 106
Kant on value of unequal
well-wishing 99
Greece *see* Aristotle; classical
antiquity; Plato
grief *see* loss of friends
Grimald, Nicholas 80
groups of friends 161–2
Guy-Bray, Stephen 150–1

Hallam, Arthur Henry 163–6
Hazlitt, William 81, 107
Héloïse and Abélard 65
Henty, George Alfred 113
Homer: *Iliad* 124–32,
140–1, 142
homosexual love in history 3, 5
Achilles and Patroclus
124–5, 154
age and *paederastia* roles
124–5, 153–4
David and Jonathan 136–8
as element in friendship 123,
138, 147, 152–7, 165
Montaigne on friendship
and 89
nineteenth-century fiction and
virtuous male friendship
114–16

Nisus and Euryalus 144–5,
146–7
Orestes and Pylades 149
and Plato's *Symposium* 20–1,
27–30
suppression in hostile societies
156–7
honour and loyalty to friends
49–50, 52, 55, 180
Hughes, Thomas: *Tom Brown*
novels 113, 115–16
Huguenots and religious conflict
85–6
humanism
and Enlightenment views of
friendship 105–6
and Renaissance thought 78,
83
Hume, David 42, 95, 100–1,
103–4, 105, 162

infatuation 118–19, 173
instrumentalism 7, 24, 25, 39,
187, 201
and false friendship 3–4, 36,
66, 176–7
and Plutarch's advice 58, 59
see also utilitarianism
intellectual exercise
Montaigne on conversation
amongst friends 84
Voltaire and Emilie
du Châtelet 101–2, 158–9
Wordsworth and Coleridge
157–8
intimacy
Kant's limitations on 99–100
and women's friendships 14
Iphigenia 147–9
irrationality 182

224

Index

Index